The Althouse Press
Faculty of Education, The University of Western Ontario
O'Neill and Norris, SCHOLARLY WRITING WORTHY OF PRINT

Scholarly Writing Worthy of Print

Gilbert Patrick O'Neill

Robin Patricia Norris

The Althouse Press

First published in Canada in 2006 by
THE ALTHOUSE PRESS
Dean: *Allen Pearson*
Director of Publications: *Greg Dickinson*
Faculty of Education, The University of Western Ontario
1137 Western Road, London, Ontario, Canada N6G 1G7

Every reasonable effort has been made to acknowledge the copyrighted material contained in this edition. If errors or omissions have occurred, necessary corrections in future editions will be made provided written notification is received by the publisher. This book is sold with the understanding that neither the authors nor the publisher is hereby rendering accounting, legal, psychological, or other professional advice. The personal services of a competent, certified professional should be sought if such advice or other expert assistance is required. Neither the authors nor the publisher is responsible (as a matter of product liability, negligence, or otherwise) for any injury resulting from any material contained herein.

Editorial Assistants: *Katherine Butson, Lois Armstrong, and Vangie Castillo*
Cover Design: *Louise Gadbois*

Library and Archives Canada Cataloguing in Publication

O'Neill, Gilbert Patrick, date
    Scholarly writing worthy of print / G. Patrick O'Neill, Robin P. Norris.

Includes bibliographical references and index.
ISBN 0-920354-59-9

    1. Academic writing--Handbooks, manuals, etc. 2. Scholarly publishing--Handbooks, manuals, etc. I. Norris, Robin P. (Robin Patricia), date II. Title.

LB2369.O64 2006   808'.027   C2005-907281-4

Printed and bound in Canada by Hignell Book Printing, 488 Burnell Street, Winnipeg, MB, Canada R3G 2B4.

This book is dedicated to all the students we have taught and mentored over the years. It is their curiosity, their joy, and their gratitude that kept us going.

Table of Contents

Figures

Preface

A good preface must be the root and the square of the book at the same time.

Friedrich Von Schlegel

This book is an advanced, writer's guide that, if consistently followed, will greatly increase your chances of getting into print. It is not a grammar handbook, a research textbook, or a style manual, although numerous references are made to all three throughout the text. The book assumes that readers have a basic command of the English language, that they know how to conduct research, and that they can follow the rules of a style manual.

We wrote the book primarily for Canadians, but it could be used in other contexts. The objective was to produce a scholarly textbook, one that can be used effectively in a variety of settings. Throughout, we strive to keep the interests of Canadian scholars at heart by using suitable Canadian examples, by retaining traditional Canadian spelling, and by citing recent Canadian sources.

The book is designed for college and university courses, but can be used constructively in writing clinics and workshops. The chapters follow a natural sequence for teaching, but the order could vary depending on students' needs. The book has a detailed subject index to help locate topics.

The book is multidisciplinary. References were deliberately taken from many fields. This approach is based on the premise that the principles of scholarly writing and publishing are universal. Good writing, for instance, is essential to getting published whether you are in the life sciences, the physical sciences, or the social sciences. Moreover, the skills, once acquired, can be easily transferred to other situations including the writing of conference abstracts, the writing of grant proposals, and the writing of professional reports.

The text is divided into nine chapters. Chapter 1 establishes the tone of the book. Chapter 2 defines scholarly writing. Chapter 3 reviews prewriting. Chapters 4 and 5 prepare the novice for writing. Chapters 6 and 7, respectively, discuss the writing and publishing of papers. Chapter 8 discusses books and reviews, and Chapter 9 discusses writing-related topics.

We believe that the book is timely given the mounting pressure on academics to publish. Clearly, times have changed. Today, careers will be quickly terminated and hopes rapidly dashed without a respectable bibliography. *Scholarly Writing Worthy of Print* provides the information, the resources, and the impetus needed to get published. We urge, therefore, that all aspiring authors add it to their library, that it be parked alongside the other indispensable tools of the profession, namely, a standard dictionary, a modern thesaurus, and an appropriate style manual.

G. Patrick O'Neill and Robin P. Norris

Acknowledgements

The authors thank the following contributors to this book:

❖ *Anne Balon* for suggesting changes to the text, for producing the camera-ready figures, and for formatting the final version of the manuscript;

❖ *Paul N. Sachis* for helping to research material for the book and for checking many of the entries in Appendix A;

❖ *Dr. Ann-Marie DiBiase* for sharing her thoughts on the contents of the book;

❖ *Elizabeth M.* and *V. Alexander Toth* for sharing their thoughts on grammar, punctuation, and word usage;

❖ *Andrew Short* for reviewing the section on grammar;

❖ *Carol Polych* for reviewing the section on Aboriginal peoples;

❖ *Carol Gaspari*, Reference Librarian at Brock University, for reviewing the section on literature searches;

❖ *Don Kinder*, Coordinator of Library Instruction at Ryerson University, for helping to research items for Appendix H;

❖ *Dr. Margaret Ann Wilkinson*, Professor, Faculty of Law and Faculty of Information and Media Studies, The University of Western Ontario, for reviewing the section on copyright law;

❖ *The reviewers* at The Althouse Press for their helpful comments and suggestions;

❖ *Katherine Butson*, Editorial Assistant and Manager of The Althouse Press, for her professional direction and support; and

❖ *Dr. Greg M. Dickinson*, Professor of Education and Director of The Althouse Press, for his guidance, patience, and encouragement. Together, we found the right words.

Chapter One

Introduction

Of all those arts in which the wise excel,
Nature's chief masterpiece is writing well.

John Sheffield, 1st Duke of
Buckingham and Normanby

Why This Book?

*W*e wrote the book for three reasons. First, we wrote it to help inexperienced writers get published. "Published works are the currency with which we purchase tenure, promotion, salary increases, and the respect of colleagues" (Olson, 1997, p. 52). But most graduate students are not taught how to write and publish; when in position, they are left to fend for themselves. Yet, clearly, writing and publishing are complex operations that need specific direction. *Scholarly Writing Worthy of Print* fosters this direction.

Second, we wrote it to clarify issues that are often misunderstood by beginning as well as established writers. For example, orders of development are often mistaken for types of writing, American spellings are often substituted for Canadian spellings, and "peer-reviewed" is often confused with "blind-reviewed." Yet, these are matters with which every writer should be familiar.

Third, we wrote it to improve the reader's writing skills. It does this by modelling. When you model, you demonstrate by example. Content informs craft; craft confirms content. Content "tells" you

1

how to write; craft "shows" you how to write. The former without the latter defeats the purpose of writing and reading about writing.

Why Write?

Academics write for many reasons; the most compelling, no doubt, are promotion and tenure. In short, it is "publish or perish" (Cantor, 1993; Day, 1998; Euben, 2002; Theilhelmer, 2003).

> Although the expression "publish or perish" has now become a cliché in academic circles, the importance of its message to faculty who desire to advance at either colleges or universities (and certainly in their disciplines) remains as strong as ever. For graduate students desiring to obtain an academic or research position, publications can provide that extra edge that sets their credentials apart from those of other candidates. (Ross & Morrison, 1993, p. 29)

Other less compelling reasons include seeing your name in print, establishing a reputation among your peers, or gaining a piece of immortality. Still others write because they wish to advance knowledge, improve practice, or share insights. Whatever your reasons, write because you want to, not because you have to.

What you want to say may not at first be evident. But this is the exciting part about writing. It is an adventure. You write to understand your own ideas, to discover yourself. Unfortunately, many novices have it backwards. They believe that they must know "exactly" what they want to say before they say it. But they are mistaken. You must wade in. You cannot wait for ideas to come to you; you must go in search of them. Say what you want to say now; fill in the blanks later. There is no other way. It is the inescapable part of being a writer.

ക്ക്ക്ക്ക

There are a thousand thoughts lying within a man that he does not know till he takes up the pen to write.

William Makepeace Thackeray

ക്ക്ക്ക്ക

Becoming a Writer

A writer is more than a person who writes. Writers are acculturated. They identify with the work of a writer. They will aspire, they will struggle, they will endure. When asked, "What do you do?", they respond, "I am a writer." Writer is their persona. It is the image that they project to the world. Some acquire image, in part, through courses; others acquire it, in part, through mentoring and modelling.

Courses can improve your writing skills, but they should not be seen as a panacea. Much depends on the syllabus. Courses, for instance, that focus on word sensitivity—semantics, syntax, and style, can help you write more clearly and effectively. However, this can be achieved only by class discussions, group exercises, and individual conferences. Avoid courses that are predominantly lecture-oriented. Absorbing knowledge is not the same as applying knowledge. A useful course will examine the works of others and help you apply the lessons learned.

The instructor should be a resource person, someone who can speak from experience. They should be the facilitator who structures the program, provides the material, and motivates the participants.

Be wary of courses that promise too much. You cannot adequately cover all aspects of writing in one semester. Hence, a worthwhile course can get you started on the road to being a writer, but the decision to become a writer is ultimately yours. Mentoring and modelling can help.

Mentoring is an intensive one-to-one form of collaboration in which an established writer (i.e., a mentor) inducts an apprentice (i.e., a student) into the writing culture of a specific group. A good mentor instructs, demonstrates, guides, and supports. The objective is to help students confront themselves as writers. The mentor achieves this in four steps. First, they talk about the writing process. What does it mean to be a writer? Why do you become a writer? How do you become a writer? The student "accepts" the challenge. Second, the mentor demonstrates by example. Together, the mentor and the student explore the hurdles of writing. The bar is raised or lowered depending on the student's fortitude. What is the expectation? How do you reach it? The student "confronts" the standard. Third, the mentor encourages reflection. They compare notes. They share insights. They exchange ideas. They affirm the norm. The student "absorbs" the culture. Fourth, the mentor fosters independence. The student assumes ownership. Ownership implies empowerment. And empowerment signals expression of self. When the community endorses their work, they embrace the community. The acceptance of the former implies the acceptance of the latter. The student "ingests" the ethos; it nurtures their image as writer.

Modelling is the reflection of significant others in self. When you model, you read as writer. When you read as writer, you observe craft. Craft is the weave. It is how a writer wields words. You look for common identities. When you find them, you bond. When you bond, you model. When you model, you imitate others. And when you imitate others, you hone craft. You become attuned to the cadence, the nuances, the resonance, and the like. You connect. You scan and you sort. You adopt and you adapt. You retain and you reject. You cultivate taste. Words become prized possessions; they become you. They build character. Character gives identity. And identity gives sense of self.

You must, however, pick your models wisely. The best examples are found in refereed journals (see Chapter 7) and in peer-reviewed books (see Chapter 8). Model those who are easy to understand. Avoid those who are hard to understand. Do not defer to them.

> When a piece of writing confuses us, we often assume that we are not up to its demands....We have seen hundreds of students experience relief from doubts about their own competence when they realize that if they are unable to understand an article or monograph, it is not necessarily because they are incompetent, but because its author couldn't [think and] write clearly. (Williams, 1990, p. xi)

Breaking Writer's Block

Writer's block is the "inability to put words on paper" (Nelson, 1993, p. 1). You cannot focus. You cannot find the right words. You cannot generate the next line. You are adrift. You have lost yourself and, in turn, your ability to write. The expression should not be confused with writer's cramp which is characterized by muscular spasms, tremors, and, occasionally, paralysis of the limbs.

There are two types of blockers: permanent and temporary. The permanently blocked cling to "the rule: Do right and fear no man, don't write and fear no critics" (Oliver, 1986, pp. 186-187).

> To put words to paper is to abandon the divine world of the possible and enter the profane world of the real, with all its trivial limitations. To take action, to write, means turning one's back on the never-never land of adolescence, where anything and everything is always about to happen, could happen, but usually never quite does happen. (Nelson, 1993, p. 76)

By imagining everything and doing nothing, they can remain "potentially great" (p. 79) for the rest of their lives. Many have built a reputation "on pipe-smoking while looking thoughtful" (Oliver, 1986, p. 186). As a group, they remain buried

> indefinitely in the data-gathering and data-assessment stages. The filling of files with quotations, statistics, and anecdotal information is virtually a vocation in itself. It is impermeably defensive. It avoids criticism and invites praise. The scholar-at-work is industrious. He is devoted. He leaves no stone unturned. There is no end to what may be learned about his chosen subject. As for thinking about it, how can he, until all the relevant data have been mastered? As for writing about it—don't be absurd. In due course, the time will come. (p. 187)

The temporarily blocked pride themselves on their writing and strive to maintain respect among their peers. Some manage block on their own while others seek therapy.

Block is normally due to a combination of three interrelated factors: procrastination, perfectionism, and self-doubt (Boice, 1990). Exactly how they interplay varies. Each case is unique because writing is unique. No two writers are identical. Thus, no two remedies are identical. The same strategy will not solve every problem nor will it work equally well for everyone. Even the most promising technique associated with each type of block may not work well for every writer. The point is, there are no cure-alls; you must experiment to find the solution that works best for you.

Procrastinators wait until the final hours, then binge. They write in marathon sessions (5 or more continuous hours in one sitting). As a result, they are always writing under extreme pressure which compounds the problem.

> When blockers do manage to write, they usually do so under the most aversive of [*sic*] conditions—amidst deadlines, fatigue, and hurried prose that invite rejection and reinstate the [conditions] that brought on blocking in the first instance. (Boice, 1993, p. 44)

The solution is balance and moderation. Procrastinators need discipline. They should find out when they write best and then write regularly (see Chapter 4). Evidence suggests that "writers who work in a regimen of regular writing, regardless of readiness or mood, produce more writing and evidence more creative ideas for writing than do writers who wait for inspiration before beginning" (p. 34).

ॐॐॐॐ

I write when I'm inspired, and I see to it that I'm inspired at nine o'clock every morning.
                                        Peter De Vries

ॐॐॐॐ

Perfectionism is caused by the "I must be perfect" syndrome, which does not allow for spontaneity, not even on the first draft. But,

> premature revising is counterproductive in various ways. When we put ourselves in a correcting, fault-finding frame of mind, we usually have more trouble coming up with new and interesting ideas. We see faults in ideas before we've had a chance to work them out, and we get distracted in our thinking by all the fixing and correcting at the surface level. Besides, premature revising usually gets us to spend time fixing or correcting things that we later throw away. Or worse yet, we don't throw away something we ought to throw away, because we've invested so much time and energy managing it that we can't bear to let it go. (Elbow, 1998, p. xxiv)

The best solution is automaticity. "Of all the cures for blocking, the oldest and most persistent are variations on automaticity.

'Automatic' means writing with a reduced awareness of what is being written" (Boice, 1993, p. 30). Automatic writing includes both spontaneous (free) writing and generative writing. Spontaneous writing is writing without conscious awareness; you let your ideas flow freely. It is rapid, uncritical, effortless writing (Boice, 1990). Sessions are short: 10 to 15 minutes. You do not preplan or stop to edit. The objective is to brainstorm on paper, to explore your thoughts and feelings, not to produce fine copy. Spontaneous writing jump-starts your brain, it gets your creative juices flowing, and it helps build momentum. It works because

> like other variants on writing unself-consciously, [it] gives people license to write without feeling responsibility for the product. That same license, of writing without conscious awareness, brings related freedoms, including the right to be playful and imperfect. (p. 51)

Generative writing is similar to spontaneous writing except that it is "product-oriented" (p. 47). Both require writing "without stopping or editing" (p. 56), but the former asks you "to write with a specific topic in mind" (p. 56). It can be practised in bouts of 10 minutes, 30 minutes, or 60 minutes depending on your endurance levels. Warm up with short, spontaneous sessions and then move to longer, generative sessions. Write first and outline second (see Chapter 3). When you finish, transform the parts into a coherent whole. This will be your first draft. "Generative writing helps establish tolerance for imperfection. By definition, writing before you're ready means that you'll be writing imperfect sentences, leaving gaps in information/analysis, and taking pressure off yourself" (p. 67).

Self-doubt is caused by negative self-talk and fear of external criticism. Negative self-talk is "the insidious voice that whispers that your best is not only not good enough but is awful, worthless, ridiculous" (Nelson, 1993, p. 49). It is inner dialogue, "roof-brain chatter" between the self and the ever-present authority figures within the self—an overly critical parent or an insensitive teacher. "Primary-level teachers get the brunt of the blame. They are recalled for undermining students' confidence as writers, for excluding playfulness from writing, and for providing little useful knowledge about ways of improving writing" (Boice, 1990, p. 11). The voice destroys the blocker's ego. It shatters their sense of self as writer. It tells them that they have nothing worth saying, and that others can say it better. Believers succumb. The prophecy is fulfilled. "Fears, like beliefs, are nearly always self-fulfilling. The subconscious 'Prover' comes into play. I'm afraid I can't write. So I don't write. Presto: the fear has fulfilled itself" (Mundis, 1991, p. 43).

There are two ways to manage the voice. First, try to win support. "Try to respond to your critic with calm agreement. You can almost always find something in the criticism that is conceivably correct, at least from the critic's perspective. Then, ask for more criticism!" (Boice, 1990, p. 102). Asking for more criticism "often helps win the critic over as a real supporter. Critics tend to respond with reassurance and compliments and with more constructive criticisms" (p. 102).

Second, try to substitute the negative self-talk with positive self-talk. Confront the voice. Take control. Refute it. Correct it. Tell it to stop the gibberish. "When blockers learned to recognize and replace their negative self-talk, they found a modest improvement in fluency and a major increase in comfort with scholarly writing" (Boice, 1993, p. 43).

Fear of external criticism arises when writers invite judgment by significant others who may be critical of their work, and by extension, themselves. There is fear that they will be rejected, found out, or appear dull. "I am a worrier and always think of how readers will object or disagree. This was the temperament that lead to my being totally blocked and unable to write for a couple of years" (Elbow, 1998, p. 122).

The solution is to stop worrying. You cannot be too sensitive and be a successful writer. Most refereed journals reject between 70 and 90 percent of all their submissions (Henson, 1997). Thus,

> most articles you read in scholarly journals *have been rejected* once, twice, or even more times before being accepted so that you can eventually read them in print. If these rejected works can eventually make it into print, it is certainly possible that yours can as well. (Thyer, 1994, pp. 57-58)

So take your critics lightly; if you are too serious or let others upset you, you will never write. You must develop a "carefree attitude," one that allows you to stand aside, from time to time, and laugh at your peers. Do not let them deter you. Be confident, take the initiative.

> If you think you can do it, you can. What you chiefly have to fear is fear itself. If you wait for inspiration—if you wait until the words pile up and simply pour forth, irresistibly and effortlessly, you will have a long wait: probably forever. (Oliver, 1986, p. 191)

Dispelling Myths

Myth 1: *Scholarly writing is art, not craft.*

Writing is both art and craft. Art is mental, craft is manual. Art is vision, craft is voice. Art is idea, image, insight. Craft is fabric, fibre, form. Each complements the other.

Myth 2: *Good writers are born, not made.*

Generally, this is an excuse for not writing. It assumes that writers are born with certain attributes that make them different from nonwriters. In other words, good writers do everything instinctively; they just know, just do, just write. But, this is untrue. Writing (the act of) is a skill, and like any other skill, the development of writing skill excellence takes practice, patience, and perseverance. Good writers are made; most are self-made.

Myth 3: *A writer is a writer is a writer.*

This is utopian. Everyone writes, but not everyone is a writer. A writer is someone who subscribes to and practises the norms of their culture. Those who subscribe to the norms, but fail to practise them, are scribblers.

A scribbler is a "very minor, untalented, or disreputable" author (Pickett et al., 2000, p. 1566). Minor means inferior. Their work is substandard. It is below their cultural norm.

Untalented means unskilled. Scribblers lack finesse. Their craft is crude. It is forced. It is rushed. It is unattended. "It is unworthy of print."

Disreputable means discreditable. Scribblers will advocate one standard, but operate by another. They will extol the virtues of brevity, for example, yet fail to exemplify it in their own work. They know the ingredients, but cannot manage the mix. That is for writers.

Myth 4: *A writer can think aloud while writing.*

A writer can think aloud (discuss his or her thoughts) while playing at writing, but a writer cannot think aloud while working at writing. A writer who "works at" writing takes the role of writer. The person (i.e., the self) and the writer (i.e., the role-taker) are one. They are fully present, fully engaged in the activity at hand (see Chapter 4). The moment you think aloud, you disengage. When you disengage, you "play at" writing. You play the role of writer. The person (i.e., the self) and the writer (i.e., the role-player) are separate entities.

When you work at writing, you are inside your thoughts (i.e., with self). When you play at writing, you are outside your thoughts (i.e., with others). You cannot be both inside and outside your thoughts at the same time. Role-takers are always inside their thoughts; role-players are always outside their thoughts. Role-players can think aloud while writing; role-takers cannot.

Myth 5: *There is only one way to write.*

Writing is an individual act. There are as many ways to write as there are individuals. There are no universal prescriptions. Students who believe that writing can be reduced to a simple algorithm have been misled. There are no magic formulas, no secret recipes, and no quick fixes.

ঌঌ৽৽

People think that I can teach them style. What stuff it all is! Have something to say, and say it as clearly as you can. That is the only secret of style.

Matthew Arnold

ঌঌ৽৽

Myth 6: *Writing is a sedentary activity.*

The act of writing (i.e., drafting) is a sedentary activity, but there is more to writing than sitting in front of a computer. Writing is part of your existence. You are always reflecting on what you have written and on what you might write. It is a 24-hour, 7-day-a-week job. Precious thoughts can come and go when you least expect them. They can occur anywhere and at any time—when running, when reading, when resting. The challenge is to catch them. Most never return.

Myth 7: *Writing is a neat activity.*

Calligraphy is a neat activity. Composition is a messy activity. The whole evolves from the parts. The parts adjust to the whole. Sentences are shaped and reshaped. Paragraphs are shuffled and reshuffled. What is to be read first can be written last; what is to be read last can be written first. What is written first need not remain last and what is written last need not remain first.

Myth 8: *You learn to write by writing.*

This is partly true, but there is more to writing than writing. Most serious writers are avid readers. They know that reading as writer teaches you the subtleties of good writing. Indeed, "studying other writers, and imitating their style, is exactly how you learn to write well yourself" (Ritchie, 1997, p. 22).

Myth 9: *"I" is forbidden in scholarly documents.*

Traditionally, this was so, but today there is no consensus. Some journals object to its use, others welcome its use. The impersonal style forces you to use phrases like: "The data were collected...," "The writer found...," or "It was discovered that...."

Proponents argue that "I" is more direct, hence, the right choice. Opponents argue that "I" is too personal, hence, the wrong choice. Understandably, where and why you use "I" is debatable, but how you use it is not. Its informal usage is different from its formal usage. Informal usage permits personal perspective. You may air your views, express your feelings, and display your biases. In contrast, formal usage is restricted by the principles of scholarship. You must remain objective (see Chapter 2). You may state a fact, but you cannot voice an opinion unless you support it with evidence. "I collected the data," is a fact. The sentence does not express an opinion or show emotion. Yet the sentence: "I believe that the planet is doomed," is an opinion. It expresses a belief and should be avoided unless it is documented.

Myth 10: *Style is just good grammar.*

Good grammar is part of style, but style is more than grammar. Style is a synergy of art, craft, and grammar. Art is the substance of thought. Craft is the expression of thought. And grammar is a system of rules that govern craft. Craft adds personality, grammar increases clarity.

Style, then, is your way of thinking and writing. It is often associated with a particular writer, thus the phrase "distinctive style."

Myth 11: *Content is more important than craft.*

This is not necessarily true. Both are important. Your work must add to the literature and your ideas must be profound. This is a given. But presentation is also important. Editors will not rewrite the manuscript for you. There is a limit to what they will tolerate when it comes to careless craft.

> Most readers are not impressed by elaborate sentence construction and excessive verbiage presented in an unorganized manner. Invariably, editors will reject a manuscript in which good material has been presented in a form that readers must work unnecessarily to understand. (Barlow, 1992, p. 244)

Myth 12: *The more sources cited, the more scholarly the document.*

Quantity alone is an inadequate indicator of scholarship. You must look at the type of source (i.e., primary vs. secondary) (see Chapter 9) and the quality of the source (i.e., refereed vs. nonrefereed) (see Chapter 7). A refereed, primary source is generally the best indicator of scholarship. A refereed, secondary source is normally the second-best indicator of scholarship. Nonrefereed sources are harder to assess. A book review (a secondary source), for instance, might be viewed as more scholarly than a government report (a primary source), but it would depend on the report. You have to ask: Who wrote it? Was it commissioned? Is there a political agenda? Is it research-based?

Myth 13: *Scholarly writing is boring.*

The word boring can refer to either the topic or the writing style. Topic, on the one hand, is relative. Few people are interested in every subject. Thus, all topics are both boring and interesting, depending on the reader. Writing style, on the other hand, is not relative. It is either lively or boring. A lively style is lean and lucid. A boring style is bloated and blurred. A boring style beclouds the message and confuses the reader. But, this is not the purpose of writing. Be wary of those who

> try to reach a higher level of distinction than their associates. This motive too often leads authors to believe that prose filled with polysyllabic and abstract words, qualifying clauses and phrases, and long sentences makes them more learned. Authors must not forget that pompous prose can also be seen as coming from an inconsiderate windbag arrogantly wasting a reader's time. (Huth, 1999, pp. 192-193)

Myth 14: *Scholarly writers are a solitary lot.*

This is a stereotype. The person is confused with the act of writing. Writing is a solitary activity, but writers may, or may not, be solitary types. Assuredly, some are, but many are not. Their membership varies. Some are activists, some are passivists, some are social, some are asocial, and so on. The point is, you cannot generalize about this group any more than you can generalize about any other group.

Myth 15: *Academics write for financial gain.*

No doubt, some do, but the majority do not. There are few, if any, direct financial incentives for publishing in periodicals. Most journals and magazines (see Appendix A) do not pay for manuscripts. In fact, you may be asked to subsidize publication costs. A $50.00 handling fee, for example, is not uncommon. Moreover, once your paper is accepted, you could be charged a publication fee. The fee is based on a schedule: so much per page (page charges), so much per figure (figure charges), so much per table (table charges), and so much for each additional reference beyond the first 10 (reference charges).

Book publishing may be profitable, but it depends on the publisher. As a rule, they take the lion's share. You are normally expected to pay for the typing and formatting ($1,000 plus), all the permissions ($1,000 plus), and the indexing ($1,000 plus). As well, you may be expected to subsidize the publisher's costs with your own money or with a grant from a sponsoring agency. Royalties, if any, typically range from 6 to 18 percent, but some companies pay no royalties on the first one thousand copies while others pay no royalties until they recover all their costs (see Chapter 8). And royalties are usually calculated as a percentage of net sales, not retail sales. Net receipts are based on the publisher's revenues after discounts and expenses. The royalties on foreign sales are even less, about one-half of the domestic rate.

Myth 16:   *Conference presentations are the best forum for sharing research results.*

Conference presentations may be the best forum for sharing interim results, but they are not the best forum for sharing conclusions. Conference presentations are preliminary reports. A preliminary report is something antecedent to something more important. It is a minor match before the main event. The main event, in this case, is a refereed, journal article. Ideally then, for every presentation, or series of presentations, there should be a corresponding publication. An imbalance (e.g., 50 presentations/5 publications) signals a failure to understand the two, time-honoured tenets of research. First,

> a scientific experiment, no matter how spectacular the results, is not completed until the results are published. In fact, the cornerstone of the philosophy of science is based on the fundamental assumption that original research *must* be published; only thus can new scientific knowledge be authenticated and then added to the existing database that we call scientific knowledge. (Day, 1998, p. ix)

And second, the scientific journal is the best vehicle for publishing research results. It is

> the repository of the accumulated knowledge in a field. In the

literature are distilled the successes and failures, the information, and the perspectives contributed by many investigators over many years. Familiarity with the literature allows an individual investigator to avoid needlessly repeating work that has been done before, to build on existing work, and in turn to contribute something new. A literature built of meticulously prepared, *carefully reviewed* [italics added] contributions thus fosters the growth of a field. (*Publication manual of the American Psychological Association*, 2001, p. 3)

Myth 17: *Conference presentations are prime candidates for publication.*

Some are; some are not. It depends on the type of paper presented. There are two types: a talk (an informal speech) and an address (a formal speech). A talk is a soapbox presentation. As a rule, there is no abstract, proposal, or outline required; the only restriction is time. There may be a short question and answer period, but there is no formal opportunity to challenge the speaker. The topic is catchy, the text is wordy, the tone is chatty. Talks are poor candidates for publication.

இருஇரு

Those who write as they speak, although they speak very well, write badly.
                                            Comte de Buffon

இருஇரு

Addresses are better candidates for publication. But again, it depends on the type of address. A keynote address, for instance, might resemble a talk. It may be more formal than a talk, but, in essence, it is still a talk. Session addresses (i.e., papers with respondents) are probably the best candidates for publication. Still, most will require extensive revisions because conference papers are rarely prescreened. The initial selection is usually based on the proposal, not the paper itself. The paper is written (sometimes hastily) after the proposal is accepted. Hence, there is little, if any, quality control over the papers. This is left to the discretion of each presenter. Published proceedings are the best incentive. Most presenters will put extra effort into papers that compete for publication.

Chapter Two

Defining Scholarly Writing

*Brilliance has an obligation not only to create
but also to communicate.*

J. R. Platt

The Four Types of Writing

*T*here are five types of writing, of which four are used extensively in scholarly writing: argumentation, description, exposition, and narration. Argumentation is sometimes confused with persuasion. The two are not the same. Argumentation depends largely on rational appeal whereas persuasion depends largely on emotional appeal. Argumentation uses fact, it strives for objectivity, and it is bound by ethical canons (see Chapter 9). Persuasion uses intuition, it is grounded in subjectivity, and it is unbound by ethical canons. Persuasion appeals to personalities (*argumentum ad hominem*), to popular opinion (*argumentum ad populum*), and to authority figures (*argumentum ad verecundiam*).

Argumentation is not arbitrary; it follows formal processes. The two basic processes are deduction and induction (Babbie, 2001; Best & Kahn, 2006; Elmes, Kantowitz, & Roediger III, 2003). Deductive reasoning is based on general truths. The line of argument is from the general to the particular. The general law is the major premise, the particular case is the minor premise, and the conclusion is the deduction. This pattern of argument is called a syllogism. Syllogisms can take different forms. The classic example is

1. All men are mortal (major premise),

2. Socrates is a man (minor premise),
3. Socrates is mortal (valid conclusion).

The validity of deduction hinges on the truth of the premises and the order of construction. If the premises are false or incomplete, and the order incorrect, the conclusion will be invalid. For example,

1. All fish live in water (major premise),
2. Dolphins live in water (minor premise),
3. Dolphins are fish (invalid conclusion).

Well-constructed syllogisms make a whole. They use official classification systems, they define their terms, and they qualify their conclusions.

Inductive reasoning uses particular facts to establish general truths. Its arguments depend on evidence derived from observation. It is sometimes called controlled induction because the conclusions are based on statistical inference. You always infer from a sample to a population. The hypotheses of induction are often formed from deductive conclusions just as the premises of deduction are often formed from inductive conclusions. This movement back and forth between induction (particular to general) and deduction (general to particular) is the fount of scientific knowledge. Their fusion is the backbone of argumentation.

Description depicts the physical features or mental state, or both, of a subject. The subject could be a person, animal, place, or thing. There are two types of description: subjective and objective. Subjective description adds a personal dimension to the subject. It is used in creative writing. Objective description focuses on the subject only. It is used in scientific writing.

Objective description can be further divided into individual or group description. Individual description, whether fixed or moving, requires order. The writer is the pivot; everything is written from their vantage point: from the closest to the farthest, from the inside to the outside, from the north to the south, and so on. If the writer moves, the description moves accordingly. For instance, you could describe the surrounding land formations as you move from point A to point B. Individual description is sometimes supplemented with a diagram (see Chapter 4). The parts or steps are usually placed in boxes, labelled, and connected with lines indicating the direction of the movement. The description then follows the logic of the flow, the course, or the operational sequence. Pertinent diagrams can present vast amounts of information, while saving text. They should not, however, stand alone. Always describe the parts, but never belabour them. Unnecessary description clogs communication.

ह∕ह∕ऽ⌐ऽ⌐

The point of good writing is knowing when to stop.

Lucy Maud Montgomery

ह∕ह∕ऽ⌐ऽ⌐

Group description divides, classifies, and labels species and objects into distinct categories according to specific criteria. The same criteria must be applied consistently to all items being classified so that each member of the group will have the same attributes. The simplest system is binary: cold/hot, dark/light, large/small, and the like. Other more sophisticated, multitiered systems are found in the medical and natural sciences.

Exposition explains and illuminates a subject. It helps the reader understand and appreciate a subject from the writer's perspective. The writer, though, must first have the term or concept clear in their mind before they can convey the meaning to others. This is best done through definition. Definition will help you clarify your subject and your thoughts about it. There are two types: restricted and extended. Restricted definitions define keywords and concepts used throughout a document. They may be either shallow or deep. A shallow definition repeats the term being defined in the definition. For example,

A scribbler is a "person who scribbles" (de Wolf et al., 2000, p. 1314).

It tells you nothing.

A deep definition states the term being defined, places it in a specific class, or subclass, and then distinguishes it from other members of that class. For instance, both a scribbler and a writer are authors, but the former is a hack, the latter is an artist. Thus, a deep definition is both inclusive and exclusive. It is inclusive because the term is placed in a specific class (i.e., author); it is exclusive because the term is differentiated from other members of that class (i.e., hack vs. artist).

Extended definition may comprise a section of a treatise or the entire treatise. Concepts are redefined through a review of the literature. The text draws on past definitions, compares and contrasts them, summarizes them, and concludes with a more comprehensive definition.

Next to definition, exemplification is the most common device used in expository writing. To exemplify means to illustrate by example. Example helps illustrate a generalization that a reader might otherwise misunderstand or question. To be effective, it must be placed next to the point it exemplifies. Examples include: a comparison (analogy, metaphor, simile), a lesson (parable), a story (anecdote), a testimonial, et cetera.

Narration is storytelling. It chronicles a series of activities, events, or scenes. The story may be told in either the first- or third-person. First-person narration brings an individual perspective to the story. You inject your thoughts and emotions into the story. It is used to write autobiographies, to recount personal experiences, and to give on-site reports. Third-person narration divorces the narrator from the story. You remain detached; the account is objective and matter-of-fact. It is used to describe laboratory experiments, to record historical events, to register natural phenomena, and to write progress reports.

Narration is temporal: Events are organized chronologically. The order is either continuous or discontinuous. For example, you could start in the present and introduce flashbacks as you work your way through the story. Or, you could start in the present, advance to the distant past, return to the present, and then gradually work your way back to the distant past. Or, you could start at the end, move to the present, and slowly work your way to the end, returning momentarily to the present at the end. The combinations are limitless, but should be limited as too many may disorient the reader.

Shifts in time are signalled by clock and calendar time, by tenses, and by transitions. Clock and calendar time is the thread that holds the sequence of events together. The story unfolds with the passage of time. Changes in events are prefaced by changes in time. Time is relative. It may be condensed or expanded. A week may seem like a day. A day may seem like a week.

Most narratives are written in the past tense, but are sometimes mixed with the present tense to create a sense of immediacy or urgency.

Transitions are connective words and phrases that hold the narrative together. Words like *after, at the same time, before, later, meanwhile, next, now, soon,* and *then,* act as signposts. They keep the reader abreast of changes in sequence and time; without them the continuity would be broken.

All written discourse or prose, no matter how it is classified (creative/scientific, fiction/nonfiction, informal/formal, literary/ technical), contains one or more of the five types of writing. Rarely would a document include only one type of writing. There are 11 scholarly combinations:

1. Argumentation, description
2. Argumentation, exposition
3. Argumentation, narration
4. Description, exposition
5. Description, narration
6. Exposition, narration
7. Argumentation, description, exposition
8. Argumentation, exposition, narration
9. Argumentation, description, narration
10. Description, exposition, narration
11. Argumentation, description, exposition, narration.

The Two Styles of Writing

The two styles of writing are informal and formal. An informal style contains

1. Unsupported opinion,
2. Subjective description,
3. Nonstandard diagrams,
4. Unofficial classification,
5. Shallow definitions, and
6. First-person narrative.

An informal style is characterized by the use of contractions; by the use of incomplete sentences; by the use of incorrect spelling (e.g., tonite); by the inconsistent use of abbreviations, capitalization, and punctuation; and by the use of labelled dictionary expressions (e.g., *colloquial* [localisms, provincialisms, regionalisms], *dialect, informal, nonstandard, slang*). See Appendix C for a list of 150 informal expressions and their formal counterparts.

A formal style contains

1. Supported opinion,
2. Objective description,
3. Standard diagrams,
4. Official classification,
5. Deep definitions, and
6. First- or third-person narrative.

A formal style is characterized by the use of full constructions; by the use of complete sentences; by the use of conventional spelling; by the consistent use of abbreviations, capitalization, and punctuation; and by the use of unlabelled dictionary expressions.

Of course, levels of informality and formality are relative. There are different degrees of informality just as there are different degrees of formality. Some styles of writing are very informal, others are very formal, and still others are borderline. Different degrees of informality are used in magazines, newspapers, and personal correspondence. Likewise, different degrees of formality are used in business reports, government documents, and scientific journals.

The Eight Principles of Scholarly Writing

Scholarly writing uses a formal style. If all writing was put on a continuum from very informal to very formal, scholarly writing would be at the formal end. There is less licence with scholarly writing than with most formal writing. The community sets the standard. Tradition controls the community. Recruits are socialized into the community through example and precedent.

ϟϟϟϟϟϟ

Culture is an instrument wielded by professors to manufacture professors, who when their turn comes will manufacture professors.

Simone Weil

ϟϟϟϟϟϟ

The tradition has eight guiding principles. All are numbered and listed separately for purposes of presentation. They should not, however, be viewed in isolation. Translated, the eight principles should be seen as complementary; all are interrelated and inseparable in contributing to the whole.

1. *Good, Scholarly Writing is Correct.* It is accurate, deliberate, proper. Words are carefully picked to convey the meaning intended. Incorrect usage is viewed as an imposition on the reader. Do not say X when you mean Y or Y when you mean X.

X	Y
agnostic	atheist
amoral	immoral
apiary	aviary
appreciate	depreciate
apprentice	intern
arbitration	mediation
bimonthly	semimonthly
centrifugal	centripetal
concave	convex
connote	denote
debut	premiere
deductive	inductive
disbeliever	nonbeliever
discovered	invented
disinterested	uninterested
farsighted	nearsighted
fraternity	sorority
honorarium	stipend
imply	infer

infertile	impotent
inhibit	prohibit
intercellular	intracellular
predecessor	successor
prescribe	proscribe
translucent	transparent

2. Good, Scholarly Writing is Clear. It is plain, simple, unadulterated. It

> is clear, not because it presents simple ideas, but because it presents ideas in the simplest form the subject permits. A clear analysis does not falsely reduce a complex problem to a simple one; it breaks the problem down into simple, comprehensible parts and discusses them, one by one, in a logical order. A clear paragraph explains one of these parts coherently, thoroughly, and in language as simple and as particular as the reader's understanding requires and the context allows. (Barnet, Stubbs, Bellanca, & Stimpson, 2003, p. 98)

The use of big words creates a barrier between writer and reader. Avoid pretentious words like antidisestablishmentarianism, disproportionateness, and other polysyllables. The rule is, never utilize (use) a big word when a smaller one will suffice (do). Technical terms are the exception. Rarely are there smaller substitutes for technical words. Thus, the use of technical language is permissible provided it is used appropriately. Appropriately means that it is restricted to specialists or defined when used with nonspecialists. When technical language is overused, it becomes jargon. Jargon goes by various names depending on the discipline or field of study. For instance, in biology, it is known as "biologese," in education, it is known as "educationalese," and, in law, it is known as "legalese."

Use "wordese" by choice, not by chance. Be aware of when, where, and why you use it. Ask yourself: Am I continually using technical terms because they convey ideas that cannot be expressed otherwise, or am I trying to impress my colleagues and friends? Initially, you may impress your friends, but assuredly, you will never impress your colleagues. So, "whatever you do, don't choose words to impress your readers. You won't" (Sides, 1999, p. 175).

3. *Good, Scholarly Writing is Concise.* It is terse, compact, succinct. There is no wordiness. Wordiness is the use of many words when few will do. It is the product of too many qualifiers, unnecessary repetition, and roundabout constructions. Most qualifiers add nothing to the meaning. Too many clutter your text, undermine your authority, and reduce your impact. Below is a list of 20 troublesome qualifiers:

a bit (of)	merely
absolutely	most certainly
a little	much more
actually	quite
awfully (informal)	rather
certainly	really
completely	really quite
definitely	somewhat
kind of (informal)	sort of (informal)
literally	very

Use them sparingly. For example,

> don't say you were a bit confused and sort of tired and a little depressed and somewhat annoyed. Be confused. Be tired. Be depressed. Be annoyed. Don't hedge your prose with little timidities. Good writing is lean and confident. (Zinsser, 2001, p. 71)

Unnecessary repetition appears in phrases like past history. The word "past" is redundant because it is inherent in the word history. History is the branch of knowledge that records past events. Words and phrases that say the same thing (twice) are called tautologies. Appendix D contains a list of 100 tautologies. The words in parentheses are redundant; omit them.

Roundabout constructions are called circumlocution. Circumlocutions are detours. They take you the long way around. Instead of saying "alone," they say "all by themselves" or instead of saying "I support...," they say "I am in favour of...." Circumlocution bloats the text, distracts the reader, and delays the message. Some phrases such as "as you know," "be that as it may," and "it can be said that" should be eliminated (altogether). Others can be reduced substantially (in size). Appendix E contains a list of 120 circumlocutions and their abridgements. Use the abridgements in your writing.

՞՞՞՞

That writer does the most, who gives his reader the most knowledge, and takes from him the least time.

Charles Caleb Colton

՞՞՞՞

4. | *Good, Scholarly Writing is Coherent.* | It is <u>bound</u>, <u>united</u>, <u>whole</u>. There is a *connectedness* <u>between</u> parts, small and large. Writing that flows smoothly from one point to another, from one sentence to another, and from one paragraph to another is coherent. Coherence is achieved by the proper use of links. There are four main links: headings, pronouns, repetition, and transitions.

Headings and subheadings mark natural intervals in the composition of your text, thereby making it easier to follow the structure of your thoughts.

Pronouns are excellent connectors because they act as substitutes for nouns that would otherwise have to be repeated. They can, however, confuse the reader if the person or thing to which they refer is unclear. There are 10 rules:

1. Use a singular pronoun when referring to a singular antecedent unless the construction is sexist (see Chapter 5).
2. Use a plural pronoun when referring to a plural antecedent.
3. Avoid sentences in which there are two possible antecedents for a pronoun.
4. Do not use a pronoun to refer to an implied noun.
5. Use a plural pronoun to refer to two or more antecedents joined by "and."
6. A compound antecedent joined by "or" or "nor" is singular if both elements are singular, and plural if both elements are plural.
7. When one of the antecedents connected by "or" or "nor" is singular and the other plural, the pronoun agrees with

the nearer antecedent.

8. A collective noun (e.g., committee, faculty, team) takes a singular pronoun unless the members act individually.

9. Use a singular pronoun when referring to the indefinite pronouns *anybody, anyone, anything, each, everybody, everyone, everything, nobody, no one, nothing, somebody, someone,* and *something,* unless the construction is sexist (see Chapter 5).

10. Use a plural pronoun when referring to the indefinite pronouns *both, few, many, others,* and *several.*

Repetition of keywords and phrases is an effective device for maintaining continuity across paragraphs. You can achieve this effect by repeating expressions at the beginning of a paragraph that were used at the end of the preceding paragraph.

Transitions act as road signs. They "give a sense of continuity that makes readers feel comfortable. As they finish one sentence, there is a logical bridge to the next" (Blicq & Moretto, 1999, p. 375). They are often placed at or near the beginning of a sentence, but can appear anywhere. Below are 100 transitional words and phrases classified according to their functions. Stagger their use because reliance on one or two favourites (e.g., also, also, also) can create tedium in your writing.

Addition:	also, and, as well, besides, further, furthermore, in addition, moreover, too
Comparison:	likewise, similarly
Concession:	admittedly, granted, of course, naturally, true
Contrast:	alternatively, but, conversely, however, in contrast, instead, nevertheless, nonetheless, on the other hand, otherwise, rather, regardless, still, though, yet
Emphasis:	after all, certainly, clearly, fortunately, here, indeed, in essence, in fact, interestingly, no doubt, of course, plainly, surely, undoubtedly

Example: for example, for instance, in particular, namely,
                    particularly, specifically, that is, to illustrate

Restatement: as stated, briefly, in brief, in effect, in other words,
                    in retrospect, in review, in short, remember, that is,
                    translated

Result: accordingly, apparently, as a result, consequently,
                    evidently, hence, so, supposedly, therefore, thus

Sequence: first, second, third...; lastly; next; some..., others...,
                    and still others...; subsequently; then; ultimately

Summary: as a rule, in conclusion, in general, in summary, in
                    total, to conclude

Time: at last, at present, at the same time, at times,
                    currently, lately, meanwhile, oftentimes, on
                    occasion, recently, sometimes, thereafter, to date

   5. *Good, Scholarly Writing is Sincere.* It is direct, frank,
straightforward. The message determines the words. If the message
is sincere, the word choice will be exact, and the message will be
explicit. If the message is insincere, the word choice will be inexact,
and the message will be implicit. Euphemisms are inexact expressions
substituted for words and phrases thought to be harsh or offensive.
Their use is normally tolerated in sensitive situations, such as death,
but they should not be used to mislead the reader. Using euphemisms
to mislead the reader is called "public lying" (Barnet et al., 2003, p.
109). Public lying avoids

> substance, direct answers, and plain words. Its tendency is to subvert
> the English language. It employs and invents euphemisms, but the
> public liar intends to protect not his listeners, but himself and his
> friends, and he misleads and deceives consciously. (p. 109)

Appendix F contains a list of 50 euphemisms and their translations.
Use the translations in your writing.

   6. *Good, Scholarly Writing is Specific.* It is categorical,
discriminating, particular. Specific refers to a member of a class.

General refers to a group or class. A specific word is definite; a general word is indefinite. Bird is general. Finch is specific. Goldfinch is more specific. Book is general. Authored book is specific. Authored, scholarly book is more specific. Specific words are vivid words. They tell the reader that you know your topic. General words are vague words. They tell the reader that you lack knowledge or refinement. Dynamic writers use specific words. Dull writers use general words.

General	Specific	More Specific
artist	painter	impressionist
beverage	beer	lager
building	house	bungalow
Christian	Protestant	Lutheran
doctor	dentist	endodontist
European	Italian	Sicilian
gun	pistol	revolver
institution	school	grade school
jewellery	ring	diamond ring
languages	Celtic	Irish Gaelic
literature	fiction	novel
publication	periodical	magazine
science	biology	zoology
technology	computer	laptop
vehicle	car	sports car

7. *Good, Scholarly Writing is Original.* It is novel, unique, refreshing. Clichés are unoriginal expressions. The word

> *cliché* comes from the French word for "stereotype," a metal plate cast from a page of type and used, before photographic printing processes, to produce multiple copies of a book or page without having to reset the type. So a **cliché** in language is an expression stamped out in duplicate to avoid the trouble of "resetting" the thought. (Lunsford, Connors, & Segal, 1995, p. 457)

Many clichés begin as slogans. They are buzzwords and catchphrases that have mass appeal. Initially, they are a novelty, but with overuse rapidly become an annoyance. They are the sign of a lazy writer (i.e., a hack); someone who relies on worn-out expressions to communicate. Appendix G contains a list of 100 clichés. Limit their use. Too many deaden thought, block creativity, and slow communication.

      8. | *Good, Scholarly Writing is Objective.* | It is rational, essential, impartial. It appeals to reason, not to emotion. Nothing should be implied or left to the reader's imagination. Folklore, guesswork, and hearsay are not permitted. Never state the opinion of others as fact, or the opinion of the majority as fact. Rely on empirical evidence, not on popular press.

ဆာဆာ

If fifty million people say a foolish thing, it is still a foolish thing.

Anatole France

ဆာဆာ

     Being objective means being honest. False reporting is unethical (see Chapter 9). You "must" be forthright. Some researchers find it hard to accept failure or negative conclusions. As a result,

> four common and serious flaws may crop up. One is to rationalize away the breakdown of the stated hypotheses and to bring in new elements not previously mentioned. Another is to extrapolate the findings and conclusions to situations and to populations not represented in the sub-populations studied. A third is to lean on the "fudge factor" to reach the expected conclusions. A fourth, and the most serious, is to draw conclusions not warranted by the findings. (Strauss, 1969, p. 168)

Remember,

> every research project has limitations and weaknesses which may or may not be the fault of the investigator. In any case, it is his obligation to be *intellectually honest* [italics added] and aware, and to point them out as a caution to the consumers of his research and as a guide for future workers in the area. (p. 168)

Honesty also means giving credit where credit is due. The purpose is twofold. First, it allows the reader to check the accuracy of your material, and second, it allows the reader to assess the quality of your material. You must acknowledge your source when

1. You quote from published or unpublished material that is not your own,
2. You quote from published material that is your own,
3. You paraphrase someone else's published or unpublished work,
4. You paraphrase your published work,
5. You copy a figure or table, in part or whole, from a source.

Quotations must be copied verbatim. They must be enclosed in either quotation marks or be blocked off from the text. The credit will vary depending on your style manual (see Appendix B). In APA format, you give the name of the author(s), the date of publication, and the page number(s). Use quotations when they

1. Lend authority to your arguments,
2. Express ideas efficiently,
3. Summarize details,
4. Provide examples,
5. Exemplify good writing.

You must, however, refrain from using too many. Use them judiciously and

> sparingly, because using them to support your ideas is one thing, allowing them to take control of your paper is quite another. Your essay belongs to you; resist the temptation of letting the authors of your sources speak for you. (Strath, Avery, & Taylor, 1993, p. 32)

Paraphrases do not normally require page numbers, but you must still credit the source. Again, check your style manual. Paraphrases are used in place of quotations when

1. The main ideas are sufficient,
2. The style is too informal,

3. The language is discriminatory (see Chapter 5),
4. The space is limited,
5. The section is written poorly.

Paraphrasing can take different forms, but must keep the main ideas. You can use some of the original words and change others, use synonyms, or abridge the passage.

Chapter Three

Preparing to Write

> *Knowledge is of two kinds. We know a subject ourselves,*
> *or we know where we can find information upon it.*
>
> Samuel Johnson

Drafting a Thesis

$\mathcal{T}$he topic you wish to advance should be one with which you are familiar or one in which you have a keen interest. It should be timely and tailored to a specific audience (see Chapter 7). Abstracting parts of your Master's thesis or doctoral dissertation and reworking the material into manuscripts is a good place to start. Some can be repackaged and published as journal articles, others can be repackaged and published as books (Harman, Montagnes, McMenemy, & Bucci, 2003). You can also publish some of the material that you gathered during your studies, but did not incorporate into the dissertation itself.

Publication requires revision. You must work your topic into a thesis. A thesis frames your vision. It tells the reader where you are going and how you are going to get there. Your first draft is called a working thesis.

> A working thesis is important for three main reasons: (1) it directs your thinking, research, and investigation and thus keeps you on track; (2) it helps you to focus on a particular point about the topic; (3) it provides concrete questions to ask about purpose and audience. (Lunsford et al., 1995, p. 23)

A thesis is often divided into two parts: a general statement and a specific statement. The former states the purpose, the latter lists questions. The purpose is to analyze, classify, compare, develop, evaluate, examine, explore, review, and so forth. The questions ask what, why, when, how, where, and who. For example,

> The purpose of this paper is to explore the option of term appointments for positions of added responsibility in the West Vancouver Secondary School System. Specifically, the paper addresses five questions:
>
> 1. What are term appointments?
> 2. Why term appointments?
> 3. Who should implement them?
> 4. How best can they be implemented?
> 5. What impact might they have on morale?

A good working thesis has three qualities.

> It is potentially *interesting* to your intended audience. In its language, it is as *specific* as possible; and it limits and focuses a topic enough to make it *manageable*. You can evaluate a working thesis by checking it against each of these criteria. (p. 24)

Searching the Literature

You should conduct a literature search if your material is outdated or your knowledge base is limited. Reviewing the literature provides new insights into a topic. It allows you to compare and contrast your observations with others and to make a unique contribution. The search can be conducted manually or by computer, or by both means. Manual searches are sometimes used initially to assess the volume of literature and to identify keywords and concepts.

The print indexes are divided into the periodical indexes and the abstract indexes. The periodical indexes list articles published in one or more fields. The periodicals included in each index are usually noted in the front of the index or in the front of the volume. The indexes are organized alphabetically either by subject heading or by subject heading and author surname. If you know people in the field, look for their surnames; otherwise, look for keywords or subject headings (index terms) that relate to your working thesis. Some indexes have a thesaurus that will help you with this step. A thesaurus is a guide that lists and cross-references subject headings used in a database. It provides synonyms, broader terms, narrower terms, and related terms. Always start with the most recent volumes. Read the bibliographical entries under each heading. If, after checking two or three volumes, you find nothing relevant, drop the heading and replace it with others. If you find a relevant title, record it onto a 3 X 5 in. bibliography card. Use cards because they are easier to handle than paper, they hold up better than paper, and they are easier to arrange and file than paper.

A separate card should be used for each entry. Always give the complete citation. Use the format (i.e., APA, CBE, MLA, etc.) required in your manuscript, including proper capitalization, proper indentation, and proper punctuation. For articles in APA format, include

1. The author's name (surname and initials),
2. The date of publication,
3. The full title of the article (no abbreviations),
4. The full title of the periodical,
5. The volume and the issue, and
6. The page numbers.

For books in APA format, include

1. The author's, compiler's (Comp.), editor's (Ed.), or translator's (Trans.) name (surname and initials),
2. The year of publication,
3. The full title of the book (no abbreviations),
4. The edition,
5. The place of publication, and
6. The publisher.

Check the APA style manual for other entries (see Appendix B).

The abstract indexes work much like the periodical indexes, but in addition, they provide summaries of the articles. They are divided into sections, each covering a different area within a discipline. The sections, in turn, are divided into an author index and a subject index. Both are listed in alphabetical order. Again, you look for keywords or index terms that relate to your working thesis. As before, you start with the most recent volumes. The abstract indexes themselves do not contain bibliographical data; rather, they list only the subject of the article. The number located at the end of each entry refers to the number of the abstract. You should copy down relevant numbers and look them up in the abstracts which are found in either a separate volume or at the front of the index volume. If the title is related, record the entry onto a 3 X 5 in. bibliography card as noted above. Be systematic and thorough. Write legibly or print clearly. Do not rush your search, as little is gained if you fail to obtain either accurate or adequate information.

෩෩෩෩

Nothing is more vulgar than haste.

Ralph Waldo Emerson

෩෩෩෩

  Examples of print periodical and abstract indexes include: *Biological Abstracts*, the *British Education Index, Dissertation Abstracts International, Index Medicus, Index to Canadian Legal Periodical Literature, Psychological Abstracts*, the *Social Science Citation Index, Sociological Abstracts*, and *Women Studies Abstracts*.

  Manual searches are useful, but can be tedious and time-consuming, particularly when your topic is broad-based, complex, or voluminous. In these situations, computer searches are recommended. As a rule, they are more flexible, less time-consuming, and, if properly executed, more efficient. For instance, the computer permits simultaneous searching of themes with more than one subject heading. And you can narrow your search to a specific author, to a specific date, or to a specific location. You can also specify the type of material you want, that is, articles, books, reports, et cetera. In addition, the computer can search titles or abstracts directly using keywords should a concept not have a subject heading. Some will even search multiple databases. This interface option is especially advantageous in fields that draw from several disciplines. As well, you can print the bibliographical citations, the abstracts, and, if it is a full-text database, the complete document.

Computer searches can be conducted from your home or from a library terminal. Home searches require an Internet connection. Check with a reference librarian for remote access instructions. A typical search involves five steps. First, select your electronic database. It could be a CD-ROM (compact disc read-only memory) database or an on-line database. Each CD-ROM contains a large volume of information. One disc, for example, could contain all the entries found in a print index spanning 10 or more years. On-line databases are stored elsewhere and must be accessed through the Internet. Usage is obtained through subscriptions. The *Gale Directory of Databases* (Mueckenheim, 2004) contains a current list (see Appendix H).

Second, select your descriptors (standard subject headings). Some databases have a thesaurus from which you choose your descriptors. You must be exact—the computer will not recognize a misspelled descriptor. Also, be sure to use American spelling for American databases. Remember, Americans use "ior", not "iour", in words like behaviour, and "er" instead of "re" in words like kilometre (see Chapter 4).

Third, plan your search. It is important to plan your search in advance because some libraries have time restrictions on terminal use and some may even charge for access time. Start your search with descriptors that most closely describe the ideas found in your working thesis. Descriptors can be combined using connecting terms called operators. There are three basic operators: *or, not,* and *and* (see Figure 3-1). The "or" operator increases the number of citations since there are more references that have one descriptor or the other than either has by itself. In contrast, the "not" operator reduces the number of citations since only references that have one descriptor, but not the other, will be selected. Likewise, the "and" operator reduces the number of citations since only references that have all the descriptors connected by "and" will be located.

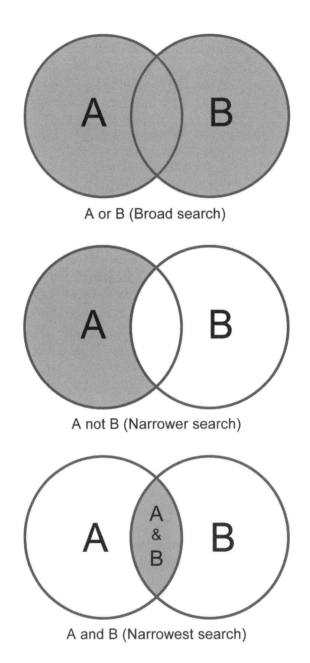

Figure 3-1. Basic search operators.

Fourth, conduct your search. You enter your search descriptors in sets or combinations using the three operators. The computer will tell you how many references there are for each search. You can reduce the number by restricting the time frame or language. For instance, you might narrow your search to the last 5 years or confine it to French.

Fifth, copy the search. You can print it, save it to a disk or your hard drive, or, depending on the database, e-mail it to yourself.

Taking Notes

At this stage, you will have a stack of bibliography cards, or a computer printout, or both. If your printout does not have abstracts, read the titles and copy those that show promise onto bibliography cards. If your printout has abstracts, read and code the importance of each entry. A typical code might be

1. For "most" important (a relevant source),
2. For "somewhat" important (a related source),
3. For "may be" important (an uncertain source), and
4. For "unimportant" (an irrelevant source).

Check your most recent references first. This strategy helps you gain insight into the area and, in turn, helps you sort out the "somewhat" and "may be" categories.

Your collection will be a mix of books, conference presentations, journal articles, reports, and so forth. The material can be acquired through your local library or through interlibrary loan. Check your library's on-line catalogue for a list of their holdings. You can search by title, author, subject, keyword(s), call number, or by International Standard Serial Number (ISSN) or International Standard Book Number (ISBN). Some documents, particularly journal articles, can be printed directly from full-text databases; others can be photocopied. Personal copies have three advantages. First, they allow you to read at your leisure; second, they allow you to make notes in the margins; and third, they allow you to highlight quotations and other important information.

Condense the rest of the material onto note cards. Use the following headings for research reports: Thesis, Method, Results, Conclusion, and Reaction. Use the following headings for conceptual documents: Thesis, Message, Conclusion, and Reaction. Use either 6 X 6 in. or 6 X 8 in. cards (see Figure 3-2). Write the call number (if there is one) in the top left-hand corner of the card and the surname(s) of the author(s) in the top middle of the card. Confine your notes to point form except for quotations. Quotations "must" be copied verbatim "with page numbers." Always double-check them. End by recording your reaction to the work. Note both strengths and limitations.

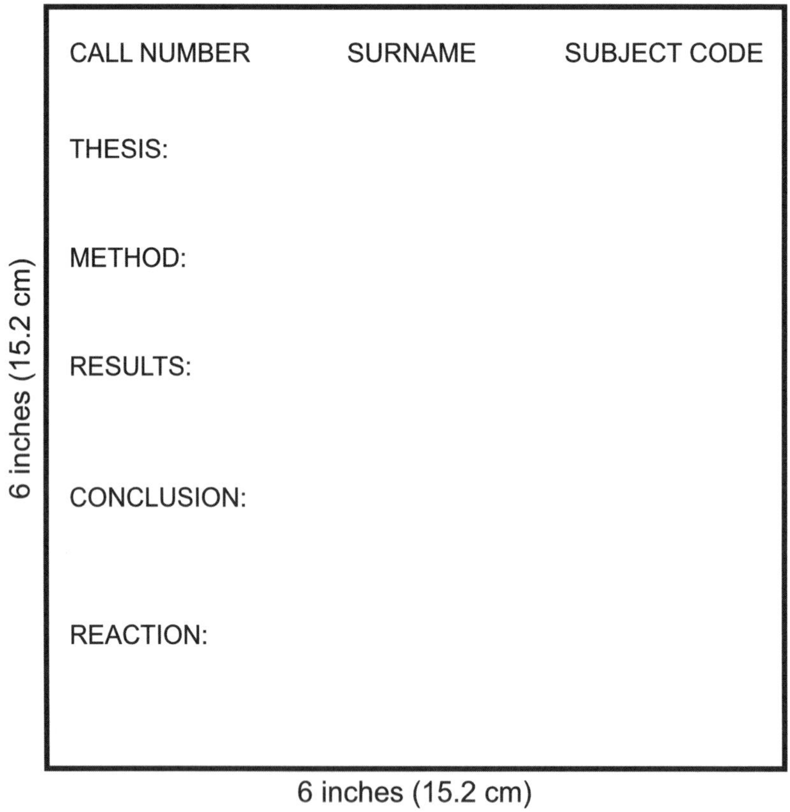

Figure 3-2. A sample note card.

Staple your bibliography and note cards together. Then, code each note card in the upper right-hand corner. Use colours, letters, or symbols. Coding has five advantages. First, the amount of research in each division or subdivision can be determined quickly. Second, studies can be easily grouped by their findings. Third, evidence for and against an argument can be amassed promptly. Fourth, outliers can be readily spotted. And fifth, the divisions and subdivisions can be transferred directly to an outline.

Profiling the Reader

Writers are frequently blinded by their familiarity with a topic and, as a result, tend to take the reader for granted. Do not make this mistake. Audience awareness is crucial to the success of any document. This awareness can be nurtured by establishing a reader profile. The profile is compiled by envisaging the primary and secondary reader.

A. Envisaging the primary reader

1. Who will be the main reader:

   ❖ administrators?
   ❖ general public?
   ❖ practitioners?
   ❖ researchers?
   ❖ students?
   ❖ theorists?

2. How much do they know about the topic?
3. How much background material is needed?
4. How much detail is needed?
5. What terms need defining?
6. What are their expectations in terms of

   ❖ style?
   ❖ structure?
   ❖ format?
   ❖ graphics?

❖ numbers?

7. What is their attitude (in general)? Are they

❖ biased/impartial?
❖ conservative/liberal?
❖ friendly/hostile?

B. Envisaging the secondary reader

1. Who will be the occasional reader?
2. How are they similar to the primary reader?
3. How are they different from the primary reader?
4. How can you accommodate the secondary reader?

Detailed responses to these questions are unnecessary, but you should sketch a profile before you start to plan and outline your document.

ॐॐॐॐ

A man really writes for an audience of about ten persons. Of course, if others like it, that is clear gain. But if those ten are satisfied, he is content.

Alfred North Whitehead

ॐॐॐॐ

Developing a Plan

Manuscripts, whether short or long, must have balance, harmony, and an orderly progression of thought that facilitates communication of ideas. Some documents may use formats in which organizational logic may not be readily apparent, but you should have it in mind before you begin writing your first draft. In short, you need a plan for dealing with the many aspects of your topic. A plan is an infrastructure—a blueprint that maps the order of development. There are 10 basic orders:

1. *Time order*
   Time order is used to record a series of events in either a continuous or discontinuous sequence (see Chapter 2).

2. *Space order*

   Space order is used to show spatial relationships: east to west, front to back, interior to exterior, left to right, near to far, top to bottom, and so on.

3. *Object order*

   Object order gives unity to loosely related themes. The text evolves around an object that is the centre of the story. An object could be a castle, a painting, a relic, a ship, et cetera.

4. *Order of increasing complexity*

   Order of increasing complexity is used to convey movement from simple to complex processes. The steps are methodical and sequential; the product is a complex operation.

5. *Order of increasing importance*

   Order of increasing importance is used to build a climax. The most important material is presented last. The order might depend on degree, size, value, and so forth.

6. *Order of decreasing importance*

   Order of decreasing importance is used to build an anticlimax. The most important material is presented first. Again, the order might depend on degree, size, value, and the like.

7. *General to particular order*

   General to particular order, also known as deductive order, starts with a premise (a global statement), makes a series of specific observations, and ends with a conclusion.

8. *Particular to general order*

   Particular to general order, also known as inductive order, builds a conclusion from a series of observations. The evidence is compiled systematically, and a tentative conclusion is drawn.

9. *Cause and effect order*

   Cause and effect order is used to explain "why" something happened or is about to happen. Evidence is compiled that helps demonstrate a relationship between two variables.

10. *Comparison and contrast order*

    Comparison and contrast order weighs the merits of two or more items; the objective is to identify similarities and differences, strengths and weaknesses, and so on.

You could have several orders of development within the same document. The main order in a journal article, for example, might be general to particular while the subsections might be a combination of time and space order. Likewise, the topics in a book might be organized in order of increasing complexity while the subtopics in each chapter might be organized in order of increasing or decreasing importance.

Constructing Outlines

An outline is a superstructure—a framework that helps divide your ideas into smaller, easier-to-manage units.   There are two types: nonlinear and linear.

Nonlinear Outlines

Nonlinear outlines are informal structures.   They go by different names (branching, clustering, mapping, etc.), but the basic concept is the same.   The focus is first on generating ideas, and second on developing structure. All nonlinear outlines start with a central theme around which they build related ideas.   The ideas are classified as either major or minor components. Major components form the main sections of your paper.   Minor components form subsections within major divisions.   Subsections can be divided into smaller units, but, initially, it is best to keep to two levels, as too much detail can clutter rather than clear your mind. The structure is established by numbering the major components, by numbering the minor components, and by drawing connections between and within major divisions.   Figure 3-3 represents a theme tree.   It was developed by

1. Writing the theme at the top of a blank page.
2. Writing, at random, and in capital letters, all major ideas that came to mind. These became the limbs of the tree.
3. Adding secondary ideas to the limbs using lower case letters. These became the branches of the tree.

4. Conducting literature searches in support of the ideas listed in 2 and 3.
5. Deleting, adding, and merging limbs and branches.

WRITER'S BLOCK

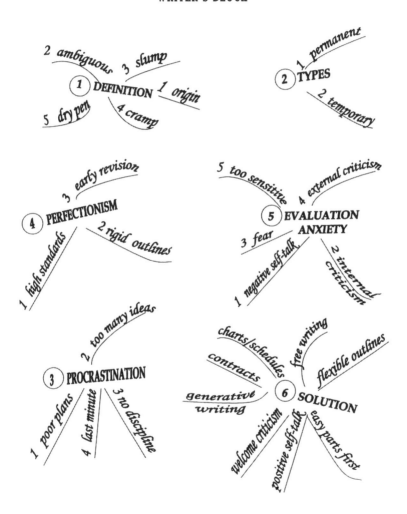

Figure 3-3. A theme tree.

The tree, as shown, contains six limbs; each limb has a minimum of two branches. The branches of the sixth limb were added later as twigs to the branches of limbs three, four, and five, thereby linking specific cures to specific causes. The order of discussion was decided by numbering the limbs and their respective branches. Not all branches were incorporated into the final draft, nor were they expected to be. Schematics refine your thinking, structure your ideas, and improve your writing. They are often used to help develop linear outlines.

Linear Outlines

Linear outlines are formal structures. They are systematic, detailed, step-by-step summaries of a subject set down in abbreviated or sentence form. There are four types: scratch, topic, sentence, and paragraph. The least complex is a scratch outline. Simply,

1. Jot down a random list of ideas. Use point form. Do not stop until you have exhausted your repertoire.
2. Study the list. Look for themes. Group your thoughts into categories. Place an A beside all the ideas that "fit" into one category, a B beside all those that fit into another category, and the like.
3. Delete irrelevant ideas.
4. Add new ideas.
5. Develop a sequence within each category. Place a 1 beside the first idea in category A, a 2 beside the second idea, et cetera. Repeat for each category.
6. Combine all your categories on separate sheets of paper. Place all the As on the first sheet, all the Bs on the second sheet, and so forth.
7. Place each category under one of the following headings:
   ❖ Introduction
   ❖ Body
   ❖ Conclusion.
8. Check for gaps in information. Earmark these sections.
9. Do additional research.
10. Fill in the blanks.

❧❧❧❧

Group the subject, the words will follow.

Cato the Elder

❧❧❧❧

A topic outline contains more information than a scratch outline. It includes a series of incomplete sentences arranged by levels of subordination. It should contain at least two major headings and several subheadings for long and complicated works. Headings are set off with numerals, letters, and indentation (see Figure 3-4). Capital Roman numerals indicate major parts. Capital letters indicate first-level subordination. Arabic numerals indicate second-level subordination. Lower case letters indicate third-level subordination and small Roman numerals indicate fourth-level subordination. Further subdivisions, although not recommended, are indicated by placing Arabic numerals, lower case letters, and small Roman numerals in parentheses.

Figure 3-4, for instance, contains three major parts (I, II, III). The second major part, the body, has three large divisions, A, B, and C, which are coordinate. A is subdivided into two components, 1 and 2. Subdivision 2 is further subdivided into three sections, a, b, and c. And b has two points, i and ii. Thus, the five sets of numbering/lettering and the four degrees of indentation give structure to the first item in the body of the paper. Notice, however, that no heading can stand alone, that is, no I without II, no A without B, no 1 without 2, and so on. If you have a single heading, eliminate it or work it into another division.

A sentence outline is similar to a topic outline. Headings and subheadings remain, but each section or subsection is summarized in one complete sentence.

A paragraph outline contains more detail than a sentence outline. Each paragraph within each section or subsection is summarized in one complete sentence. Hence, a section that has five paragraphs would have five sentences. It is sometimes called the *zero draft*, the draft before the first draft.

The type of outline you choose will depend on your skills as a writer. Some writers need much detail, others need little. As a rule, though, the more detailed the outline, the easier the writing. But, do not waste time on an outline that is more complicated than the paper itself.

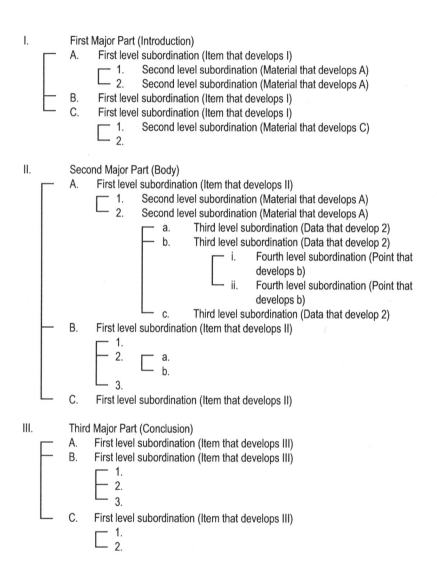

I.   First Major Part (Introduction)
    A.   First level subordination (Item that develops I)
        1.   Second level subordination (Material that develops A)
        2.   Second level subordination (Material that develops A)
    B.   First level subordination (Item that develops I)
    C.   First level subordination (Item that develops I)
        1.   Second level subordination (Material that develops C)
        2.

II.   Second Major Part (Body)
    A.   First level subordination (Item that develops II)
        1.   Second level subordination (Material that develops A)
        2.   Second level subordination (Material that develops A)
            a.   Third level subordination (Data that develop 2)
            b.   Third level subordination (Data that develop 2)
                i.   Fourth level subordination (Point that develops b)
                ii.   Fourth level subordination (Point that develops b)
            c.   Third level subordination (Data that develop 2)
    B.   First level subordination (Item that develops II)
        1.
        2.   a.
            b.
        3.
    C.   First level subordination (Item that develops II)

III. Third Major Part (Conclusion)
    A.   First level subordination (Item that develops III)
    B.   First level subordination (Item that develops III)
        1.
        2.
        3.
    C.   First level subordination (Item that develops III)
        1.
        2.

Figure 3-4. An example of a topic outline.

An outline is only a means to an end, not an end in itself. Don't view it as being cast in concrete. Outlines are preliminary by their nature. If you suddenly see a better way to organize your material while you are writing the draft, *depart from your outline and follow the better approach* [italics added]. The main purpose of the outline is to bring order and shape to your writing *before* you begin to write the draft. (Brusaw, Alred, & Oliu, 1997, p. 417)

Always test your outline before you write from it. Ask yourself:

1. Are my headings and subheadings clear?
2. Are the levels of subordination consistent?
3. Is there a logical progression? What is it?
4. Is there a balanced relationship among the parts?
5. Can I begin writing without interruption?

Chapter Four

Writing Tips 1

Like stones, words are laborious and unforgiving, and the fitting of them together, like the fitting of stones, demands great patience and strength of purpose and particular skill.

Edmund Morrison

Initiating the Novice

Securing a Sanctum

Writing requires clear thinking. "Clear thinking becomes clear writing; one can't exist without the other. It's impossible for a muddy thinker to write good English" (Zinsser, 2001, p. 9). Noise is the great enemy of clear thinking. Isolate yourself; lock your doors and record your messages. Please do not disturb! S'il vous plaît ne pas déranger. If necessary, check into a motel, rent a cabin, or buy a hideaway.

Do not compromise your work station. Pick a room with proper lighting, with plenty of work space, and with a window on the world. You need reliable equipment and other paraphernalia such as file folders, note pads, paper clips, red pens, whiteout, and so on. As well, arm yourself with a standard dictionary, a modern thesaurus, and an appropriate style manual (see Appendix B).

Running Away

Nothing is harder than those first few words. You loathe the thought. Thirty minutes and five false starts. Time passes. Tension mounts. You are not ready. You need more time. Perhaps tomorrow, but, for many, tomorrow never comes.

> There's no getting around it. That first encounter with the blank page is a terrible, anxiety-ridden moment, a nerve-racking trial at any point in a writer's life. It is possibly hardest, however, for the person either new to writing or returning after an extended absence. For the beginner, the paralysis that comes from starting cold is usually a "developmental" phenomenon, as the child psychologists say; with time and practice, it often subsides to a tolerable (though still trying) level of anxiety. (Nelson, 1993, p. 13)

This is a critical juncture at which many would-be writers falter. They have their notes, their outlines, and their tools, but they fail to persevere. Every time they sit down to write

> other tasks that have been waiting for months suddenly seem urgent; neglected disagreeable duties develop immediate appeal; and plans hitherto nebulous demand instant action. Anything—daydreaming, desk-cleaning, boss-baiting—serves to postpone writing. No dodger is more artful than a reluctant writer, and the most artful dodgers of all are the occasional writers. (Tichy, 1988, p. 9)

Writing avoidance manifests itself in many ways. Some will conduct endless searches. Others will type their note cards and still others will revamp their outlines over and over *ad nauseam*. Some will even buy a new computer, believing that it will somehow write for them, that it is indeed the missing link. But experienced writers do not fool themselves. They know that

> the computer can do only a few things well, and they're not the most important things. The computer can't think, and it certainly can't write. It specializes in minor housekeeping chores, such as moving things from one place in a document to another or changing all the uppercase letters to lowercase. It is patient, obedient, and very fast. Like a faithful dog that loves to fetch a stick for hours on end, the

computer can find any set of letters you ask it to. The problem is, however, that you have to know what letters you want it to find. And once you've got them, you have to know what to do with them. (Markel, 1994, p. 40)

It is the "wannabe" writer, not fully committed to the struggle, who looks for a miracle. In desperation, they turn to technology for magic it cannot deliver.

Others, battling commitments on their time, put everything on hold until they take their holidays. Initially, this ploy may ease their conscience, but, in the long run, it is self-defeating.

> The single most common mistake in setting up a writing schedule—one that, unbelievably, even experienced writers con themselves into committing—is to announce proudly, "Well, my schedule is too full at the moment to do any writing, unfortunately. But come semester break/summer vacation/retirement/Christmas, I will have eight hours a day to write, write, write!" Surely no faster way to trigger inner resistance has yet been devised by humankind. Comes the long-awaited time, the eager neophyte sits down at her desk and—nothing. (Nelson, 1993, p. 20)

Why? Writing, like all activities, "requires regular practice for ease of performance. The less you do, the harder it gets" (p. 21). These tactics are escape mechanisms, deadly traps into which many prospective writers fall. There is a time for everything. There is a time to research, to read, to reflect, and to write. Now is the time to write.

Facing Reality

Every aspiring writer must confront three indisputable facts. First, good writing is hard work. It requires dedication, determination, and discipline. The image may be glamorous, but the work is mundane. You must learn to hunger for the struggle, not for the fame.

彽彽彽彽

Writing isn't hard. It isn't any harder than ditch-digging.

Patrick Dennis

彽彽彽彽

Second, writing is a solitary activity. "Although you might brainstorm ideas in a group or solicit sections of a document from other people, the process of sitting down to write calls for periods of solitary confinement" (Alley, 1996, p. 229). The writer must enter a chamber—a chair, a desk, and a computer. There are no coworkers, there are no work orders, and there is no work-to-rule. You are on your own. There is only the humming of electric currents in your brain, and sometimes there are not many of these.

This is the moment of truth. You are face to face with yourself. There is no one else, you are alone, and you alone must decide. Either you are a writer, or you are not a writer. If you are not a writer, you will abandon ship. If you are a writer, you will stay the course. You will show courage. You will drop your guard. You will focus on the present. Your surroundings will become distant. The solitude will no longer matter. Your presence is all that will matter. You will be spending time with yourself. When you experience self, you go beyond your surroundings. You enter the realm of pure consciousness which is the true essence of self. Time stands still. You are fully present, fully engaged in the activity at hand. You become your work. Your work becomes you.

Solitude is the catalyst. It fuels concentration. Concentration is the path to being present. Being present is the path to finding yourself. And finding yourself is the path to being a writer. If you cannot find yourself, you cannot be a writer.

Third, writing is time-consuming. You cannot write a publishable paper in one or two sittings. There are few, if any, writers capable of working this quickly. As a rule, those who write most skilfully do so most painstakingly. All good writing is rewriting. You must write and rewrite until you get it right. There are no shortcuts. Three or four drafts are not uncommon.

> Rewriting is the essence of writing well: it's where the game is won or lost. That idea is hard to accept. We all have an emotional equity in our first draft; we can't believe that it wasn't born perfect. But the odds are close to 100 percent that it wasn't. (Zinsser, 2001, p. 84)

Getting Started

Relax. Clear your mind. Take a deep breath. Stretch. Touch your toes. Dismiss the world. Then,

> **sit down and start writing.** If you have the ideas but do not know how to express them, start writing anyway. Resist the temptation to check your e-mail, to make a cup of coffee, or to call your mother. Now is *not* the time to do your laundry or to make your bed. Sit down and start putting one word after another. (Barnet et al., 2003, p. 4)

Forget about structure, syntax, and spelling. You can attend to these matters later. Your objective is to build a "rough draft (no matter how 'rough' it is), so that when you stop for a break you know you have written something you can work up into a presentable document" (Blicq & Moretto, 1999, p. 12).

Some writers use letters or symbols to support their writing. For instance, you might use

1. Q to indicate the need for quotations,
2. + to indicate the need for examples, and
3. ? to indicate the need for references.

The point is, do not revise as you write. Writing and revision are two separate functions.

> They cannot be done simultaneously without the one lessening the effectiveness of the other. Writing calls for creativity and total immersion in the subject so that the words tumble out in a constant flow. Revision calls for lucidity and logic, which force a writer to reason and query the suitability of the words he or she has written. The first requires exclusion of every thought but the subject; the second demands an objectivity that constantly challenges the material from the reader's point of view. Writers who try to correct their work as they write soon become frustrated, for creativity and objectivity are constantly fighting for control of their fingers. (p. 12)

Keep a note pad at your side. Do not trust your memory. As

thoughts emerge, jot them down, set them aside—screen them later. Jotting is cathartic. It clears your mind. A clear mind spawns clear thinking. Clear thinking produces clear writing.

Keep going. Save successive drafts on the computer's hard drive, and on a disk or CD-ROM. Number and label them. Do not stop until you have generated at least two full pages. The text will have flaws, but that is to be expected. You have a start and that was your objective. Take a break.

Devising a System

If you are going to take your writing seriously, you must develop productive strategies that will help you meet your goals. The following six steps will do that. First, find out when you write best. Are you a morning or a night person? Initially, you can experiment, but ultimately you will have to devise a schedule that works best for you. Mornings are recommended because you can

> take advantage of your clarity of mind and higher energy. The normal activities of the day will eventually drain your energy and blunt your mental faculties. It is possible to write at day's end, after job and other responsibilities have been acquitted, and some do. But you'll give yourself a significant advantage by sitting down to it when you are fresh. (Mundis, 1991, p. 68)

Second, learn how to budget your time effectively. The most common excuse for not writing is "lack of time" (Boice, 1990, p. 13). Everyone is busy. When do you find the time? The answer lies in self-management. Set up a schedule. Replace some of your less important activities, like watching television or window-shopping, with writing time. Writing should not be done only when you feel like it, or when you have nothing better to do. Rather, it must be seen as a job, to be taken seriously, to be worked at according to set time intervals— so many hours a day, so many days a week, so many weeks a year. Start with about 6 hours a week. You can gradually increase your commitment, but be reasonable because "writing is energy-intensive.

Overreaching invites burnout and block" (Mundis, 1991, p. 67). Keep your sessions short: 2 to 3 hours.

> When you keep the writing sessions relatively brief and spread them out over several days, you not only prevent the fatigue that leads to wasted effort, but you also give your mind a chance to work on the project while you take a break....Your brain never shuts down, and sometimes it does its best work when you're not pestering it. Therefore, if you spread out the writing over several days, you increase the chance that your brain will figure out what to do while you're taking it easy. (Markel, 1994, p. 14)

Third, learn how to pace yourself. Find the speed at which you work best, then stay with it. Set a quota. The amount need not be large. One thousand words (about four pages) per sitting is realistic. If initially this is too much, lower your expectations. It is better to leave each session with a sense of accomplishment, however small, than a sense of failure.

Fourth, reward yourself for your successes, but never punish yourself for your failures. Set short- and long-term goals. Track your progress. Keep weekly charts. Use a point system. Pages equal points. Five pages equal five points. Five points buy a lunch. Ten points buy a dinner. Fifty points buy a holiday. Earn bonus points. Five extra pages, ten bonus points. Watch your points grow. Watch your writing grow.

Fifth, never permit yourself a sense of completion until the document is finished. Always stop each session in midsentence or midparagraph. Resuming at this point is much easier because it forces you to read and reread the preceding text until you recapture the flow.

Sixth, know when to quit. When you are blocked, walk away. Take a break. After an hour, try again. You cannot force writing, but you can continually put yourself in a position where it may come. And it will! If you are still blocked, revert to less taxing chores. Draw your figures, construct your tables, or compile your references. These mechanical chores, which are often seen as a nuisance, can provide relief and a sense of progress.

Sharpening Your Skills

ೠೠೠೠ

Writing is like a good watch—it should run smoothly and have no extra parts.

William Zinsser

ೠೠೠೠ

Activate Passives

Verbs have two voices: active and passive. A sentence is written in the active voice when the subject acts. A sentence is written in the passive voice when the subject is acted upon. "Rahul hit the ball" is the active voice. "The ball was hit by Rahul" is the passive voice. Passive sentences are longer because the passive voice always includes a form of the verb "to be" and a "by somebody" or a "by something" phrase. You learn "to whom or to what" something was done, then "what was done," and finally "who or what did what to what was done." The order is (a) object (receiver), (b) verb (action), (c) subject (actor). The active sequence is (a) subject (actor), (b) verb (action), (c) object (receiver). It is more direct; hence, the preferred choice when the actor is known or the actor is more important than the receiver.

Resuscitate Verbs

A smothered verb is created when a working verb is changed to a noun by adding suffixes such as *-ance, -ation,* and *-ment.* Examples include:

advance to advancement	implement to implementation
determine to determination	maintain to maintenance
develop to development	negotiate to negotiation
document to documentation	perform to performance
establish to establishment	rely to reliance

The verb is smothered because you must add a form of the verb "to be" to complete the sentence. But, there is no action in the verb to be (is, are, was, were, can be, could be, will be, has been, have been, etc.). For example,

1. Confirmation of the sabbatical was given by Dean Stein.
2. Dean Stein confirmed the sabbatical.

Confirmation is a noun derived from the verb confirm. The second construction is better because it has fewer words (5 vs. 9). It has fewer words because it uses the active voice and a working verb.

Strong, working verbs are the key to energy-filled writing. They are the engines that make words jump, sentences skip, and text flow. Smothered verbs may sound impressive, but they are not. Avoid them.

Control -ize

Verb-forming suffixes, like "-ize," are easy to construct and thus easy to use. Careless writers simply take a noun, add "-ize" to the ending, and use it as a verb. They animalize, humanize, idealize, journalize, materialize, and totalize everything. Their writing becomes an endless litany of "-ize" constructions. Use them wisely. You might, for example, alphabetize, capitalize, italicize, or standardize, but you would rarely acronymize, hyphenize, jargonize, or synonymize.

Position Modifiers

Misplaced modifiers are words, phrases, or clauses that modify the wrong word. As a result, the meaning is changed. Changing the placement will correct the meaning. For instance,

1. Lee *almost* lost all his life savings in the fire.
2. Lee lost *almost* all his life savings in the fire.

The first sentence suggests that Lee nearly lost all his life savings, but did not. The second sentence suggests that Lee did indeed lose nearly all his life savings. It is a subtle change in structure, but a substantial change in meaning. Always let the meaning determine the word order.

Dangling modifiers are phrases separated from the element that they are supposed to modify. As a result, the meaning is distorted. They usually appear at the beginning of a sentence. Rearranging the words in a sentence will restore the meaning. For example,

Rising over the hills, the hikers observed the full moon.

The placement of the participial phrase at the beginning of the sentence suggests that the hikers were rising over the hills. The hikers were probably standing still; it is the moon that was rising over the hills. Therefore, the sentence should read,

The hikers observed the full moon rising over the hills.

Always place phrases next to or near the word or words that they are intended to modify.

Squinting modifiers are modifiers that are placed between two sentence elements, either of which they could modify. The reader is left to decide: Do they modify the elements before them or do they modify the elements after them? For instance,

Mohammed was certain *by June* he would graduate.

Was he certain by June, or would he graduate by June? It can be corrected by adding "that" before or after the modifier to clarify the meaning.

1. Mohammed was certain *that* by June he would graduate.
2. Mohammed was certain by June *that* he would graduate.

৵৵৵৵

Good writers are those who keep the language efficient. That is to say, keep it accurate, keep it clear.

Ezra Pound

৵৵৵৵

Eliminate Noun Strings

A noun string is a chain of nouns, each modifying another noun. The practice is grammatically correct, but it becomes confusing when you have too many nouns. The reader has to pause to determine which words or group of words relate to one another. For example,

> The power recovery nutrition improvement high school program was implemented successfully by the government.

Program is the word modified by the long noun string, but the rest of the sentence is unclear. You can sometimes untangle a chain by

1. Using the active voice (i.e., reverse the order),
2. Using working verbs,
3. Using hyphens (e.g., low-cost),
4. Replacing nouns with adjectives or adverbs, and
5. Using prepositions (by, for, in, of, on, with, etc.).

The best approach, however, is to refrain from using them. Follow the rule: Never use more than two nouns to modify another noun, compound or otherwise.

Omit Needless Negatives

Double negatives are nonstandard English. They are redundant constructions when used to express a single negation. The use of two negatives in the same sentence produces an affirmative. Examples include:

1. No, I do not mind.
2. I cannot say that I would not have done the same.
3. The weather is not bad.
4. He is not afraid of nobody (nothing).
5. It is not as if we do not wash them.

You have to be careful, especially with words that begin with negative prefixes. Adding the adverb "not," for instance, to the following words would create a double negative:

not *anti*establishment	means	proestablishment
not *dis*satisfied		satisfied
not *extra*marital		marital
not *im*patient		patient
not *in*competent		competent
not *il*literate		literate
not *ir*reversible		reversible
not *mis*trusted		trusted
not *non*linear		linear
not *un*skilled		skilled.

"Not," however, is sometimes used to form a conditional positive. For example, it may be used before an adjective having a negative sense when the meaning intended expresses a shade of distinction not contained in the positive sense of the word (e.g., It is not uncommon to...).

  "Barely" (not much, virtually nothing), "hardly" (almost not), and "scarcely" (probably not much) sometimes create confusion. "She could not barely" means that "She could easily," which is the opposite of "She could barely."

Maintain Parallel Structures

Parallel structure is the systematic arrangement of sentences so that elements of equal grammatical function have equal grammatical form. It is achieved by repeating the same form of a word, phrase, or clause in a sentence. The first word, phrase, or clause always establishes the pattern. For instance, if the first verbal in a sentence is a gerund, then the rest of the verbals in the same sentence must also be gerunds. Examples include:

1. *My sister,* (my) *brother,* and (my) *uncle* attended the convocation. [repeated noun with possessive pronoun]

2. The doctor described the patient's problems clear*ly* and frank*ly*. [repeated adverb]
3. His duties include collect*ing*, classify*ing*, and collat*ing* documents. [repeated gerund]
4. Yadira likes *to interview* clients, (*to*) *assess* their needs, and (*to*) *offer* advice. [repeated infinitive]
5. New hockey teams were established *in Sydney*, (*in*) *Sudbury*, and (*in*) *Saskatoon*. [repeated prepositional phrase]
6. Laurier was a great leader *who spoke for the people, who fought for the people*, and *who died for the people*. [repeated adjective clause]

Parallel structure can also be used effectively in headings, illustrations, lists, and outlines. The technique is useful because it

1. Saves words (reduces clutter),
2. Equates ideas (adds symmetry),
3. Clarifies relationships (improves readability), and
4. Unifies concepts (increases coherence).

Balance Paragraphs

After the opening paragraph, each paragraph should be arranged so that it leads systematically and progressively to the closing paragraph. Unity is your guiding principle. There must be unity within and across paragraphs. Unity within demands that every paragraph have oneness of thought, that every sentence composing the paragraph bear upon a central idea. The central idea is stated or implied in the topic sentence. It is usually the first sentence of the paragraph, but it may appear anywhere.

A paragraph, then, is an entity in itself; it contains a beginning, a middle, and an end. Each sentence must be related to the one before and the one to follow. They must be balanced in themselves and in relation to one another.

Sentences have structure and papers have structure; they need structure if readers are to grasp without too much work what they have to say. Paragraphs need structure too. The start of a paragraph should seem to be aimed toward a point; through the middle the reader should sense that the paragraph is moving to that point; at its close the point should have been reached. How you give the reader this sense of movement from a start through mid-ground to a finish depends on the subject of the paragraph. (Huth, 1999, p. 176)

☙☙☙☙

Good writers are sticklers for continuity. They never allow themselves to write a sentence that is not manifestly connected to the ones immediately preceding and following it.

John Trimble

☙☙☙☙

The length of your paragraphs should vary. Although there are no rules on length, a well-developed one does not normally exceed 15 lines (Alley, 1996). A paragraph, though, can be as short as one or two sentences provided that it serves a purpose. The point is, avoid a series of short, choppy paragraphs or a series of long, complicated ones.

> Achieving effective paragraph length is part of the art of writing. For each work a writer should weigh the relative importance of the demands of the subject, format, readers' preferences, need for variety, considerations of emphasis, and effect on style. Many writers judge these subconsciously. Those who have never thought about paragraph length may have to weigh and choose consciously for a time, but soon they too will plan effective lengths without much conscious effort. (Tichy, 1988, p. 338)

Perhaps, "the best advice is that a paragraph should be just long enough to deal adequately with the central ideas stated in its topic sentence. A new paragraph should begin whenever the subject changes significantly" (Oliu, Brusaw, Alred, & Scott, 1994, p. 46).

Unity across paragraphs is achieved by arranging the parts according to your outline (see Chapter 3). Your paragraphs must be structured so that there is continuity of thought from start to finish. If you have trouble ordering your paragraphs, print them out on separate pages. Then spread the copies out on a flat surface and move them around until you are satisfied with the order. As you follow your outline, you are in essence testing it, just as you test your paper, by comparing it with your outline for it. When you finish, ask yourself six questions:

1. Is the order correct?
2. Is it logical (easy to follow)?
3. Are there gaps?
4. Are the parts interconnected (how)?
5. Are the transitions smooth?
6. Is there a sense of completion?

Curb Inconsistencies

Inconsistencies reduce the impact of a scholarly document, thereby rendering it less effective. They distract the reader, disrupt the flow, and decrease comprehension. Consistency is achieved through established conventions which dictate uniformity in construction, style, spelling, and format.

In Construction

Inconsistencies in construction are due to sudden shifts in mood, number, person, tense, and voice. Verb form determines mood. It can be indicative (expresses facts or opinions, or asks questions), imperative (issues commands), or subjunctive (expresses wishes or conditions contrary to fact). As a rule, you should not shift moods in the same sentence. For instance,

Collect the sample and it should be analyzed.

Use the imperative only,

Collect and analyze the sample.

Or, use the indicative only,

The sample should be collected and (it should be) analyzed.

Number is the quantity indicated by a noun or pronoun. It can be either singular or plural. Singular nouns take singular verbs. Plural nouns take plural verbs. Pronouns must agree in number with their antecedents (see Chapter 2), unless the language is sexist (see Chapter 5). If you have a choice between singular and plural, use the plural.

There are three persons in the English language: first person, second person, and third person. The first person is the person or persons speaking (I or we). The second person is the person or persons spoken to (you). And the third person is the person or thing spoken about (he, she, it, they). The use of the third person is encouraged in scholarly writing although the first person is becoming more widely accepted (see Chapter 1). The first person is used mainly in diaries, logbooks, and personal essays. If you begin a narrative in the first person, end in the first person. If you begin a narrative in the third person, end in the third person (see Chapter 2).

The tense of a verb determines the time of action. There are only two tenses that can function alone as main verbs in English: the simple present and the simple past. All other main verbs are verb phrases. A verb phrase consists of an auxiliary (helping) verb (be, do, have, may, must, will, etc.) and a verbal (infinitive, present participle, past participle). There are three verb phrases in the present tense: present progressive, present perfect, present perfect progressive. There are three verb phrases in the past tense: past progressive, past perfect, past perfect progressive. And there are four verb phrases in the future tense: simple future, future progressive, future perfect, future perfect progressive. Research papers switch between tenses. The following are typical:

Abstract	simple past, simple present, present progressive
Introduction	simple present, present perfect
Literature Review	simple past, present perfect
Method(s)	simple past
Results	simple past
Summary	simple past

Discussion	simple present, present progressive, present perfect, simple past, simple future
Recommendations	simple present, present perfect, simple past, simple future.

Conceptual papers vary (see Chapter 6). Historical accounts and literature reviews, for example, are written mostly in the past tense. Others might use a combination of past, present, and future tense. Too many tenses, though, can be confusing. The simple past is the safest tense.

Voice is tied closely to person. The use of the first person is associated with the active voice whereas use of the third person is associated with the passive voice. Shifts in voice are awkward. For instance,

> We can shift voices, but they should never be shifted in the same sentence.

Use the active voice only,

> We can shift voices, but (we should) never (shift them) in the same sentence.

Or, use the passive voice only,

> Shifts in voice can be used, but (they should) never (be used) in the same sentence.

In Style

Style refers to level of formality. Basically, there are two levels: informal and formal (see Chapter 2). Informal level uses a personal writing style. Formal level uses an impersonal writing style. Informal style is used in novels, plays, and short stories. Formal style is used in legal contracts, research reports, and technical documents. Use a formal style.

In Spelling

Spelling in Canada is controversial. Do you use the American or Canadian version? Unfortunately, there are no official guidelines. It is best, therefore, to use the Canadian version when submitting manuscripts to Canadian publishers and the American version when submitting manuscripts to American publishers. Switching back and forth, however, can be a problem. How do you remember which is which? Is it defence or defense? Is it syllabuses or syllabi?

Appendix I contains a list of 50 different Canadian and American spellings. The list was devised using *The Canadian Oxford Dictionary* and the *Merriam-Webster's Collegiate Dictionary* (see Appendix B). Screening and selection included three steps:

1. Each word was checked in *The Canadian Oxford Dictionary*.
2. Each word was checked in the *Merriam-Webster's Collegiate Dictionary*.
3. If the spelling of the *main headword* (i.e., the first word listed) was variant in the two dictionaries, the word was added to the list.

In Format

Consistency in book and journal format is achieved through the use of style manuals (see Appendix B). The Author Information page in a journal will tell you what style manual to use (see Chapter 7). They provide instructions on how to prepare your manuscript. Included are sections on capitalization, citations, headings, illustrations, numbering, punctuation, spelling, typing, and so on. Your work must conform to the publisher's guidelines or you risk rejection. Some multilanguage journals, though, particularly those in Europe, offer no instructions to authors. You can use whatever format you like as long as you are consistent. The consistent use of abbreviations, illustrations, and lists is sometimes a challenge.

Abbreviations. Abbreviations are shortened forms of words or phrases that stand for the whole. Their use is sometimes permitted in abstracts (check your style manual), but they should never be used in the title of a journal article or book. They should be used "only" when the primary reader will understand them (see Chapter 3). A list of standard abbreviations is given in *The Canadian Dictionary of Abbreviations* and in the *Acronyms, Initialisms and Abbreviations Dictionary* (see Appendix B). If there is more than one usage, be consistent (Sabin, Millar, Sine, & Strashok, 1999). For example, do not use "USA" and "U.S.A." in the same document. Nonstandard abbreviations should be constructed only when a term is used repeatedly. The convention is

1. Spell out the term when first used;
2. Place the abbreviation after the term in parentheses;
3. Thereafter, use the abbreviation.

The following guidelines apply to the use of standard and nonstandard abbreviations:

1. A period is placed after most abbreviations. Exceptions include acronyms (e.g., NAFTA), initialisms (e.g., YMCA), metric units (e.g., m), and points of a compass (e.g., N).
2. A word which is capitalized when spelled out is usually capitalized when abbreviated. For instance, write "Btu" for British thermal unit, "C" for Celsius, "F" for Fahrenheit, and "K" for Kelvin. Exceptions include "C" for centigrade, "ID" for inside diameter, and "OD" for outside diameter.
3. Do not add a period to the end of a sentence that ends with an abbreviation unless the abbreviation has no period (e.g., cm., but not Ltd..).
4. The plural of most abbreviations is formed by adding an "s" (e.g., nos.). Exceptions include imperial units of measurement (e.g., 1 lb. or 10 lb.), metric units of measurement (e.g., 1 kg or 10 kg), and

cc.	copies
ff.	and the following pages
ll.	lines
nn.	notes (footnotes)
pp.	pages
ss.	sections

5. Units of measurement are abbreviated only when used with numerals. For example, write "10 in." or "300 km", but not "ten in." or "several km."

6. Titles, like Admiral (Adm.), Honourable (Hon.), President (Pres.), Professor (Prof.), Senator (Sen.), and the like, may be abbreviated when the given name or initials precede the surname. For instance, write "Professor Lalancette", "Prof. Catherine Lalancette", or "Prof. C. Lalancette", but not "Prof. Lalancette."

7. Never abbreviate the names of cities, countries, provinces, regions, or states. Exceptions include the United Kingdom (UK) and the United States of America (USA).

8. Abbreviations for the Canadian (Can./Cdn.) provinces and territories and the American states and territories should be used only in addresses and references. Below are two lists. The first list contains postal abbreviations for the Canadian provinces and territories. The second list contains postal abbreviations for the states and territories of the United States. Note that periods are not used with either.

Canada

Alberta	AB	Nunavut	NU
British Columbia	BC	Ontario	ON
Manitoba	MB	Prince Edward Island	PE
New Brunswick	NB	Quebec	QC
Newfoundland & Labrador	NL	Saskatchewan	SK
Northwest Territories	NT	Yukon Territory	YT
Nova Scotia	NS		

United States

Alabama	AL	Missouri	MO
Alaska	AK	Montana	MT
American Samoa	AS	Nebraska	NE
Arizona	AZ	Nevada	NV
Arkansas	AR	New Hampshire	NH
California	CA	New Jersey	NJ
Colorado	CO	New Mexico	NM
Connecticut	CT	New York	NY
Delaware	DE	North Carolina	NC
District of		North Dakota	ND
Columbia	DC	Ohio	OH
Federated States		Oklahoma	OK
of Micronesia	FM	Oregon	OR
Florida	FL	Palau	PW
Georgia	GA	Pennsylvania	PA
Guam	GU	Puerto Rico	PR
Hawaii	HI	Rhode Island	RI
Idaho	ID	South Carolina	SC
Illinois	IL	South Dakota	SD
Indiana	IN	Tennessee	TN
Iowa	IA	Texas	TX
Kansas	KS	Utah	UT
Kentucky	KY	Vermont	VT
Louisiana	LA	Virginia	VA
Maine	ME	Virgin Islands	VI
Marshall Islands	MH	Washington	WA
Maryland	MD	Washington, DC	DC
Massachusetts	MA	West Virginia	WV
Michigan	MI	Wisconsin	WI
Minnesota	MN	Wyoming	WY
Mississippi	MS		

9. Words like Avenue (Ave.), Boulevard (Blvd.), Court (Ct.), Drive (Dr.), Place (Pl.), Square (Sq.), and Street (St.) should not be abbreviated in text, but may be abbreviated in addresses.

10. Words like Brothers (Bros.), Company (Co.), Corporation (Corp.), Incorporated (Inc.), and Limited (Ltd.) should not be used unless they are part of a proper name. Likewise, the ampersand (&), in a title, should be used only when it is part of a proper name (e.g., Arnold Todd & Sons, Inc.).

11. Abbreviations for government agencies and other familiar organizations may be used in text and references (e.g., CBC, CFL, RCMP, UAW).

12. Abbreviations for scientific, technical, and other commonly used terms may be used in text and references if the primary readership understands them. Examples include:

ABD	all but dissertation
AIDS	acquired immunodeficiency syndrome
DDT	dichlorodiphenyltrichloroethane
DNA	deoxyribonucleic acid
ESP	extrasensory perception
HIV	human immunodeficiency virus
PCB	polychlorinated biphenyl
REM	rapid eye movements
RT	reaction time

13. Never abbreviate days, weeks, months, or years in text (e.g., on Sunday, 2 weeks, August 1, 20 years). Exceptions include B.C.E. (Before the Common Era) and A.D. (Anno Domini or in the year of the Lord) when used with specific dates (e.g., 44 B.C.E. and A.D. 30).

14. Never abbreviate time (seconds, minutes, hours) in text (e.g., 10 seconds, 2 minutes, 1600 hours). Exceptions include a.m. (before noon) and p.m. (after noon) when used with specific numerals (e.g., 8:00 a.m. and 2:30 p.m.).

15. Two standard abbreviations, et al. (and others) and no. (number), may sometimes be used both inside and outside parentheses. Others may be used only inside

parentheses. Examples include:

anon.	anonymous
c.	copy
c. (ca.)	about, circa
cf.	compare
col.	column
e.g.	for example
esp.	especially
etc.	and so forth, and so on, and the like
fig.	figure
i.e.	that is
l.	line
ms.	manuscript
n.b.	note well, take note
p.	page
para.	paragraph
s. (sec.)	section
viz.	namely
vs.	versus
&	and

Exception: Legal text uses v. for versus both inside (Tennessee v. Scopes, 1925) and outside parentheses: Tennessee v. Scopes (1925).

16. Standard abbreviations may be used in footnotes, endnotes, and reference lists. Examples include:

art.	article
bk.	book
ch. (chap.)	chapter
cf.	compare
comp.	compiled by, compiler, compilation
dir.	directed by, director
diss.	dissertation
Ed.	Editor

ed.	edited by, edition
et al.	and others
f.	and the following page
ibid.	in the same place
loc. cit.	in the place cited
n.	note (footnote)
n.d.	no date (given)
no.	number
n.p.	no publisher (given)
n. pag.	no pagination
op. cit.	in the work cited
p.	page
par. (para.)	paragraph
pt.	part
pub. (publ.)	published by, publisher, publication
repr.	reprinted by, reprint
rev.	revised by, revision
rev. ed.	revised edition
3rd ed.	third edition
suppl.	supplement
trans.	translated by, translator
v.	see
vol.	volume
&	and

Illustrations. Illustrations, sometimes called graphics, refer to the nontextual parts of a document. They help clarify images that are too complex to be conveyed by words only. They provide eye relief, increase interest, reinforce ideas, and encourage comparisons. Illustrations should never stand alone. They should supplement the text, not replace it. Always state your ideas first and then reinforce them with reference to an illustration. A good illustration

1. Contains only essential information,
2. Complements rather than repeats the text,
3. Is visually pleasing to the eye,

4. Is self-explanatory,
5. Is camera-ready.

There are two types of illustrations: figures and tables. Figures include charts, graphs, and maps (Harris, 1999). Charts are diagrams that show relationships between the parts of a system or the sequence of steps in a process. The former are called organizational charts, the latter are called flow charts. The parts or steps are usually placed in boxes, labelled, and connected with lines indicating the direction of movement. Solid lines indicate direct relationships; dotted lines indicate indirect relationships.

Graphs are diagrams that show cycles and trends, but obscure discrete data points. There are three main kinds of graphs: bar (column), line (curve), and circle (pie). Bar graphs are useful for showing the parts as they relate to the whole at different times or at the same time. Differences are shown in the bar length; the width remains constant. Line graphs show the relationship between an independent variable, plotted along the horizontal axis (abscissa) and a dependent variable, plotted along the vertical axis (ordinate). Line graphs allow for easy comparison of continuous data. Circle graphs are used to show percentage distribution of the whole. The wedge-shaped sections of the pie show how the items are distributed. Information usually proceeds in a clockwise direction beginning at 12 o'clock.

Maps depict geographic features (mountains, rivers, valleys), resource distribution (primary, secondary, tertiary), or spatial distribution (rural, urban, suburban). A map should reveal its location, its scale, and its orientation (i.e., points of a compass).

Tables are the most economical way to present a large body of quantitative data. Tables, unlike graphs, emphasize discrete data points. The arrangement of data points into rows and columns facilitates comparison. Tables can also be used to present nonnumerical data. Parallel descriptions, for example, are sometimes listed in tabular form.

Organization is the key to well-constructed tables. Always arrange your row and column headings in some logical order—alphabetical, chronological, geographical, and the like (Harris, 1999). The left-hand column of a table, called the *stub*, contains the row headings (Aaa, Bbb, etc.) (see Figure 4-1). They identify items about which data are given in the rows in the body of the table. Above the stub is the *stubhead*. The stubhead (Xxx) identifies the row headings in the stub. The column headings (Eee, Fff, etc.) are located at the top of the table. They identify items about which data are given in the columns in the body of the table.

Capitalize the first word and proper nouns in all headings. Place the units of measurement (degrees, kilograms, percentages, etc.) in the headings. Use standard abbreviations and symbols.

Table 0-0. (Table number)
Parts of a Table.* (Table title)

		Xxx	Eee(%)	Fff(%)	Ggg(%)	Hhh(%)		Column Headings
Rule	→							
Stubhead		Xxx	Eee(%)	Fff(%)	Ggg(%)	Hhh(%)	←	Column Headings
Stub		Aaa	00.00**			00.00		
Row headings	→	Bbb	00.00			—		
		Ccc	—		BODY	00.00		
		Ddd	00.00			00.00		
Rule	→							
Column totals	→	Total	00.00			00.00		
Footnotes	→	* These data are confined to....						
		** Decimals rounded to....						
Source line	→	Source: From *Higher Education in the North* (p. 242) by A. N. Snow. Copyright © 2005 by Yukon Publications, Inc. Reprinted (or adapted) by permission of Yukon Publications, Inc., Whitehorse, YT.						

Figure 4-1. Parts of a table.

Numbers in the body are aligned by decimal points. When decimal points are missing, alignment is by the farthest right numeral. Blank spaces are filled with dashes (—).

Horizontal lines (rules) separate (a) the title from the stubhead and column headings, (b) the stubhead and the column headings from the row headings and the body, (c) row headings and the body from the column totals, and (d) the column totals from the footnotes and source.

Footnotes are used to help explain headings and data in the body of the table. Lower-case letters (a, b, c) or nonnumerical symbols (*, +, #) should be used, as superscript numbers can be mistaken for exponents. You must acknowledge the source if the table is borrowed in whole (reprinted) or in part (adapted) (see Figure 4-1).

Style manuals will give you instructions on how to prepare and present illustrations. If directions are unclear, use the following guidelines:

1. Title each illustration.
2. Keep your title brief.
3. Number each illustration.
4. Left justify the number and title "above" each table (e.g., Table 1. *Title*).
5. Left justify the number and title "below" each figure (e.g., *Figure 1.* Title).
6. Number your figures and tables separately.
7. Number your figures and tables consecutively.
8. Position the illustration to read from left to right and from top to bottom.
9. Leave plenty of white space.
10. Keep the construction and design consistent with other illustrations in the document.
11. Keep your terminology in text and illustrations consistent.
12. Always mention an illustration in text before it is presented.
13. Position each illustration as close as possible to the text reference, preferably on the same page or on the page after.
14. Triple-space above and below an illustration if it appears on a page with text.
15. Refer to each illustration by its number when used in context (e.g., see Table 1, not see the above table).
16. Refer to each illustration by its number and page when used out of context (e.g., see Figure 1, p. 33).

17. When a table is split between two pages, write "continued" at the bottom of the first page and repeat all headings and the number at the top of the second page (e.g., Table 2 continued).
18. Do not over-illustrate.

Lists. Lists can be a welcome relief from standard text. They are used to

1. Ask a series of questions,
2. Chronicle a narrative,
3. Describe steps in a process,
4. Explain instructions,
5. Outline criteria,
6. Provide examples,
7. Record data,
8. Report data,
9. Review facts, and
10. Summarize limitations and recommendations.

Every list should be as short as possible. The minimum number of items is two; the maximum number is indefinite. Long lists are sometimes grouped as in an outline (see Chapter 3). You may use either bullets or numbers. Numbers are best for ranks and sequences. Indent the list ½ in. from the left margin, and hang your bullets or numbers.

Use parallel words, phrases, or clauses. Capitalization and punctuation vary. Check your style manual (see Appendix B). If instructions are missing or unclear, model examples or use this text as a guide.

Chapter Five

Writing Tips 2

Great writers are significant in terms of the human awareness they promote.

F. R. Leavis

Discriminatory and Nondiscriminatory Language

*D*iscriminatory language makes false assumptions about individuals and groups based on cultural and physical characteristics. In contrast, nondiscriminatory language accurately reflects the diversity of society by acknowledging the experiences, lifestyles, and values of a wide variety of individuals and groups. It uses words and phrases that are encouraging rather than discouraging, inclusive rather than exclusive, and positive rather than negative. Nondiscriminatory language includes both nonsexist and prominority language.

Nonsexist Language

Sexist language is defined as that which reflects and perpetuates attitudes which subordinate or limit people based on their gender. It

> is written or verbal communication that differentiates between the sexes in an unfair or irrelevant manner, making direct or indirect reference to one sex when the writer or reader should address both sexes (or the other sex). (Franklin and Marshall College Writing Center and Women Aware, 1986, p. 1)

Nonsexist language promotes and maintains fairness and equality. It "discourage(s) usage that ignores or demeans women, reinforces bias and stereotypes, or focuses inappropriately on gender" (Frank & Treichler, 1989, p. 123).

The following guidelines are intended to help writers identify and eliminate sexist language in their writing. The guidelines are divided into five parts:

1. The generic man, in general,
2. The generic man, in particular,
3. Parallel gender,
4. Gender-specific pronouns, and
5. Sexist citations.

ह्ल्हल्कर्कर

We believe the concern for words that are gender-tagged is the most important shift in English usage in the last 400 years.

Anne Soukhanov

ह्ल्हल्कर्कर

The Generic Man, in General

The generic man, in general, should be used only when it refers to the adult male. It is a false generic because it excludes women. "People in general are not all of the male gender, and the usage of generic 'man' and the vocabulary emanating from it tends to perpetuate the 'invisibility' of women in the social system" (Canadian Advisory Council on the Status of Women, 1984, p. 2). Always use nonsexist words that accurately and fairly represent both sexes. Below is a list of 10 sexist expressions and their nonsexist substitutes. Use the nonsexist substitutes in your writing.

Sexist Expressions	*Nonsexist Substitutes*
average/common man	average person, people in general

gentleman's agreement	informal agreement, unwritten agreement, verbal contract
layman's terms	informal language, nontechnical terms
man/mankind	civilization, human beings, humanity, humankind, men and women, people
man (verb)	operate, run, staff
man-made	handmade, machine-made, manufactured, synthetic
manpower	human resources, labour, personnel, workers, workforce
middleman	agent, arbitrator, broker, liaison, mediator, trader
modern man	modern civilization, modern society, people today
working man	employee, labourer, wage earner, worker

The Generic Man, in Particular

The generic man, in particular, applies to titles that make distinctions between men and women. Titles that incorporate the words *boy*, *girl*, *man*, *woman*, and so on, are archaic. Today, equality should be reflected in all titles. There are three ways to maintain this equality.

First, avoid the use of titles with feminine suffixes such as *-ess*, *-ette*, *-enne*. They belittle women by giving the impression that the male term is the main set while the female term is the subset. Below is a list of six sexist titles and their inclusive substitutes. Use the inclusive titles in your writing.

Sexist Titles	*Inclusive Titles*
bachelorette	single woman
comedienne	comedian, entertainer
poetess	poet
stewardess	flight attendant
usherette	usher
waitress	waiter

Second, use either a *general inclusive* title or a *specific inclusive* title for positions that either women or men can fulfil. Examples include:

Sexist Titles	*Inclusive Titles*
businessman/ businesswoman	general: business executive, entrepreneur, manager
	specific: architect, landscaper, pawnbroker
chairman/ chairwoman	general: administrator, chairperson, department head, facilitator
	specific: Chair of the Chemistry Department
clergyman	general: clergy
	specific: bishop, imam, minister, priest, rabbi
craftsman/ craftswoman	general: artisan, handcrafter
	specific: potter, weaver, woodcarver

deliveryman	general: courier, messenger, porter
	specific: Dominion Parcel deliverer
foreman	general: inspector, leader, manager, overseer
	specific: truck assembly line supervisor
meter man (utilities)	general: meter reader
	specific: gas meter reader
repairman	general: repairer, technician
	specific: automobile mechanic, electrician, stone mason
spokesman	general: advocate, lobbyist, representative
	specific: spokesperson for the Canadian Union of Public Employees
statesman	general: diplomat, politician, public figure
	specific: Prime Minister Pearson, Senator Margaret MacKenzie Gall

Third, acknowledge the position rather than the position holder. The position may be either "general" or "specific." Examples include:

Position Holder	Position
career woman	general: professional
	specific: accountant, physicist, veterinarian
chorus girl/boy	general: cast member, chorus member
	specific: dancer, singer
headmaster/ headmistress	general: chief administrator, director, principal
	specific: Head of St. Andrews College
female athlete	general: athlete
	specific: boxer, diver, marathon runner
male secretary	general: secretary
	specific: legal secretary

Exception: The position holder is sometimes used in a comparison (e.g., On average, female golfers make less than male golfers.).

Parallel Gender

Parallel gender ensures that roles of equal function have equal emphasis and form. There are three ways to achieve this balance in your writing.

First, use equivalent constructions when presenting men and women in similar roles. Do not identify women in terms of their roles as *daughter, mother, wife*, and so forth, unless this information is significant or paired with similar references to men. Examples include:

Nonparallel Gender	*Parallel Gender*
Casey Balon, his wife and daughters	Casey and Anne Balon and their daughters Kaitlyn and Lauren Balon
ladies and men	ladies and gentlemen women and men
Nicholas and his mother	Nicholas and his mother Schenley
nurses and their husbands	nurses and their spouses
woman and husband	woman and man wife and husband

Second, address both women and men the same way. If you address a man by his given name, address a woman by her given name. If you use a woman's given name and surname, use a man's given name and surname. If initials and surname are used for one, use initials and surname for the other. If you address a woman by her title, address a man by his title. Examples include:

Nonparallel Gender	*Parallel Gender*
Teacher M. Norris and Steve Swarbrick	Meredith and Steve Meredith Norris and Steve Swarbrick M. Norris and S. Swarbrick Teacher Meredith Norris and business executive Steve Swarbrick

Third, avoid describing women in terms of their physical characteristics while describing men in terms of their mental attributes or professional achievements. Examples include:

Nonparallel Gender	*Parallel Gender*
Tenor Gerry Burnie and his beautiful aunt Mina	Tenor Gerry Burnie and soprano Mina Pogue
	Handsome, tenor Gerry Bryan Burnie and beautiful, soprano Mina Priscilla Pogue

Gender-Specific Pronouns

Gender-specific third-person singular pronouns should be avoided when the person in question is unspecified. There are many ways to do this; ten are given.

1. Use the plural form. This is the simplest and most common approach. For example,

The voter casts "her" ballot.	Voters cast "their" ballots.

2. Use a plural pronoun (*they, them, their, theirs*) after a singular noun or pronoun (*anybody, everybody, somebody*, etc.) when used in a singular, but inclusive sense. For instance,

Every grammarian has "his" list of dos and don'ts.	Every grammarian has "their" list of dos and don'ts.
Everyone should have "her" immunization updated.	Everyone should have "their" immunization updated.

3. Remove the pronoun. For example,

The manager evaluates "his" staff.	The manager evaluates staff.

4. Replace the pronoun with an article (*a*, *an*, *the*). For instance,

The stockbroker counsels "his" clients.	The stockbroker counsels "the" clients.

5. Replace the pronoun with a neutral word (*individual*, *one*). For example,

The consumer voices "her" objection.	The consumer voices an "individual" objection.

6. Replace the pronoun with a first-person pronoun (*I*, *we*). For instance,

A student can earn extra money if "he" works overtime.	I can earn extra money if "I" work overtime.

7. Replace the pronoun with a second-person pronoun (*you*, *your*). For example,

A person's academic standing depends on "her" grade-point average.	Your academic standing depends on "your" grade-point average.

8. Replace the pronoun with a combination of both masculine and feminine pronouns (e.g., *he or she*, *his or her*, but preferably not he/she or his/her). If you use this option, vary the order within the document. For instance,

Each writer must edit "his" manuscript.	Each writer must edit "his or her" manuscript.
Each writer must edit "her" manuscript.	Each writer must edit "her or his" manuscript.

9. Use the passive voice. For example,

| Every hunter should register "his" firearms. | Firearms should be registered by every hunter. |

10. Use *he* and *she* as generic pronouns in odd and even chapters respectively. Explain the convention in a footnote.

Sexist Citations

As a rule, sexist reference materials should be avoided. If, however, the material is essential, use one of the following options:

1. Quote part of the material. Reword the sexist section without changing the meaning.
2. Replace sexist words or phrases with an ellipsis (...).
3. Paraphrase the section.

ร∂∽ร∂∽๙∂∽๙๑

If you are a thinker, you will change the language. You will not use words the way others do.

Gertrude Stein

ร∂∽ร∂∽๙∂∽๙๑

Prominority Language

A minority group is a group that differs from other members of the larger society. Prominority language depicts these groups in a positive and precise way. Prominority language is "not narrow and prescriptive; it does not aim to create a canon of 'politically correct' words. It aims instead to clarify and distinguish, to move away from labelling and name-calling" (Doyle, 1995, p. 5). Four minority groups are discussed in this section: Aboriginal people(s), people with disabilities, ethnic minorities, and sexual minorities.

Aboriginal People(s)

This section is divided into four parts: the Aboriginal people in general, the First Nations, the Inuit, and the Métis.

The word *Aboriginal* means the original inhabitants of a country and their descendants. According to the *Constitution Act, 1982*, the Indians, Inuit, and Métis are the Aboriginal people of Canada (Funston & Meehan, 1994). But, the term Indian is no longer used by many Aboriginal people. They prefer to call themselves First Nations (Royal Commission on Aboriginal Peoples, 1996; Smylie, 2000). You should use the following designations when writing about First Nations, Inuit, and Métis individually or collectively: Aboriginal people(s) or Aboriginal people(s) in Canada, First people(s) or First people(s) in Canada, Indigenous people(s) or Indigenous people(s) in Canada, Native people(s) or Native people(s) in Canada (Fee & McAlpine, 1997).

The word *people* refers to "a group of individuals," "the entire body of Aboriginal persons," or a "particular group." The word *peoples* "always refers to a number of such groups, not a number of individuals" (p. 5). Capitalize the adjectives Aboriginal, First, Indigenous, and Native "to parallel other broad ethnic, linguistic, and geographic designations such as *Asian, Hispanic,* and *Nordic*" (p. 5).

The term *First Nations* refers to those communities who share a common language, identity, and heritage. When writing about a specific person or group, adopt the Aboriginal nation or tribal affiliation that the First Nations people use to identify themselves (Smylie, 2000). Examples include: an Anishnabe teacher from Wikwemikong First Nation; Buffy Sainte-Marie, a Cree singer and songwriter; a fishing crisis at the Burnt Church and Indian Brook First Nations.

The plural noun *Inuit*, meaning "the people", is the collective name for the Aboriginal people who dwell in the Arctic and sub-Arctic regions of Canada. The singular of Inuit is Inuk. Do "not" use the outdated word Eskimo to refer to the Inuit. It should be used only in historical references. Identify groups of Inuit according to the four principal settlement areas or by specific communities within each settlement area. The four principal settlement areas are Inuvialuit (western Arctic), Labrador, Nunavik (northern Quebec), and Nunavut (eastern Arctic). Nunavut, in turn, includes three separate settlement areas: Kitikmeot (central Arctic), Kivalliq (Keewatin), and Qikiqtaaluk

(Baffin) (Cragg, Czarnecki, Phillips, & Vanderlinden, 2000).

The term *Métis*, not *Metis*, is both an adjective and noun in singular and plural form. It has both an exclusive and inclusive definition depending on who is using it. When used exclusively, the term refers to people with First Nations (e.g., Cree, Ojibwa) and European (e.g., English, French, Scottish) ancestry. They are descendants of the historic *New Nation* that emerged from Manitoba's Red River Settlement in the early nineteenth century with a distinct culture, language, political will, and economic role as buffalo hunters and provisioners (McMillan, 1995; Sawchuk, 1998). Today, these people call themselves the Métis Nation.

When used inclusively, the term can refer either to those who trace their origins to the historic Métis Nation or to those of both Aboriginal and non-Aboriginal ancestry, who identify themselves socially and culturally as Métis, and are accepted as Métis by Métis communities in various parts of Canada. Examples include the Acadian Métis and the Labrador Métis.

People With Disabilities

People with disabilities are sometimes misunderstood. This section suggests four ways to write sensitively about people with disabilities.

ᚿᚿᚾᚾ

There are worse words than cuss words, there are words that hurt.

Tillie Olsen

ᚿᚿᚾᚾ

First, distinguish between the terms *disability* and *handicap*. A disability is a condition; a handicap is a barrier. A disability is a functional limitation that interferes with activities of daily living (i.e., seeing, talking, walking). A handicap is an attitudinal, environmental, legal, or societal obstacle that interferes with independence and limits participation. A handicap, then, is a barrier to a person with a disability (Gastel, 1998; Human Resources Development Canada, Office for

Disability Issues, 2002; Maggio, 1997).

Second, focus on the person, not the disability. Follow the *people first rule* founded by the disability rights movement. By putting people first you avoid language that equates the person with a condition. The individual should be seen as a whole person, not as a disability. Below is a list of eight expressions. The first list puts the condition first, the second list puts the person first. Use the "person first" list in your writing.

Condition First	*Person First*
autistics	children with autism
blind (the)	man with a visual impairment, person who is blind, woman who has low vision
cardiacs	individuals with heart disease
deaf (the), deaf-mute, deaf and dumb	person who is deaf, (the) Deaf (a distinct cultural group who identify with and participate in the language, culture, and community of Deaf people based on one of the world's sign languages [e.g., American Sign Language])
disabled (the), disabled person	person with a disability
handicapped (the)	child with a disability, people with disabilities
hard of hearing (the), hearing impaired	man who is hard of hearing, individuals with hearing loss
ostomate	woman who has an ileostomy

Third, choose descriptors that emphasize *adaptation* rather than victimization. Portraying a person with a disability "as a victim, may reinforce negative stereotypes of passivity and helplessness" (Schwartz & The Task Force on Bias-Free Language of the Association of American University Presses, 1995, p. 76). Below is a list of six expressions. The first list stresses victimization, the second list stresses adaptation. Use the "adaptation" list in your writing.

Victimization	*Adaptation*
afflicted with AIDS	prominent lawyer with AIDS
deformed by arthritis	veteran teacher who has arthritis
stricken with Parkinson's disease	actor with Parkinson's disease
stroke victim	marathon runner who had a stroke
suffering from asthma	Olympic swimmer who has asthma
wheelchair-bound	basketball player who uses a wheelchair

Fourth, replace disrespectful expressions with *respectful* expressions. Below is a list of eight expressions. The first list contains disrespectful expressions, the second list contains respectful expressions. Use the "respectful" list in your writing.

Disrespectful Expressions	*Respectful Expressions*
birth defect, congenital abnormality, deformed	baby born with a cleft lip and palate, person with cerebral palsy

brain-damaged	hockey player who has a brain injury
crazy, insane, mad, maniac, mental	child with an obsessive-compulsive disorder, writer who has depression
cripple	doctor who walks with a cane, reporter who has paraplegia
demented	grandfather who has Alzheimer's disease
dwarf (except in medical context), midget	person of short stature
invalid	person with a disability
mentally defective, mongoloid	child who has a developmental disability, adult with Down syndrome

Ethnic Minorities

The word *ethnic* refers to the sense of identity which comes from membership in a group.

> Ethnic groups consist of a kinship-based community of individuals with a shared awareness of a common identity and cultural symbols. Key characteristics include (1) a common ancestry, (2) awareness of a historical past, (3) identification with select cultural elements as symbolic of their peoplehood, (4) a set of related experiences, interests, history, origins, and descent, (5) the potential to interact with others up to and including the point of a community, and (6) a self-awareness of themselves as a "people." The viability and persistence of an ethnic group as a community depend to some degree on the level of boundary maintenance, cultural strength, institutional completeness, and shared interests. (Fleras & Elliott, 2003, p. 380)

Use the following guidelines when writing about ethnic groups:

1. Be specific. Identify ethnic groups by specific countries of origin, not by general categories that imply cultural homogeneity (e.g., Caribbean, South Asian). Canadian of Caribbean origin is general. Canadian of Jamaican descent or Jamaican Canadian is specific. Canadian of South Asian origin is general. Canadian of Sri Lankan descent or Sri Lankan Canadian is specific.

2. Be nonjudgmental. Avoid the expressions backward, Third World, and underdeveloped when referring to nations, and the expressions deprived, disadvantaged, and underprivileged when referring to groups. "Children of a particular racial or ethnic group, for example, are not culturally deprived, educationally disadvantaged, or underprivileged, except perhaps in comparison to some implicit, putative norm" (Schwartz & The Task Force on Bias-Free Language of the Association of American University Presses, 1995, p. 50).

3. Be inclusive. Use a variety of names in diverse situations, and make sure that the spelling is correct and consistent.

4. Be genuine. Gratuitous praise hurts. Adjectives "such as *well-dressed, intelligent, articulate,* and *qualified*—e.g., *qualified minorities are encouraged to apply*—may be unacceptably patronizing in some contexts, as are positive stereotypes— the polite, hard-working Japanese person or the silver-tongued Irish person" (p. 51).

5. Be relevant. Avoid references to ethnic affiliation, especially when they add nothing relevant to the message. For instance, "Izul Achmadi, an Indonesian student, was accused of plagiarism." The appositive, "an Indonesian student," in this case, is irrelevant. It serves no purpose other than to defame the group. A group should not be stigmatized by its members.

6. Be sensitive. Use "preferred designations," and do not assume group consensus. Phrases such as people of colour, man of colour, and woman of colour may be acceptable to some groups, but not to others. When in doubt, ask. "Call people what they want to be called—and accept that this may vary from group to group" (Maggio, 1992, p. 50).

ॐॐॐॐ

Good words are worth much and cost little.

George Herbert

ॐॐॐॐ

Sexual Minorities

Sexual minorities include bisexuals, gay men, lesbians, and transsexuals. The phrase *sexual orientation* refers to sexual identity. Sometimes it is confused with the term *sexual preference.*

> "Preference" implies that homosexuality, bisexuality, transsexuality, and heterosexuality are casually chosen rather than crucial, given, inextricable aspects of one's identity. Sexual orientation is not synonymous with sexual behavior; one's sexual identity is just that— who one is, not what one does. (Maggio, 1997, p. 360)

The word *gay*, when used as an adjective or noun, refers to people with same-sex emotional and sexual orientation, or to those who identify themselves as members of the gay community. The term is preferred by gays and lesbians to the more clinical word homosexual because gay is cultural and social as well as sexual. Some older gays, however, may still identify with the word homosexual. Although the term gay can refer to either gay men or to gay men and women, it usually refers to men. The preferred designation for women of same-sex orientation is "lesbian." It is best, then, to use the preferred expressions, lesbians and gay men or gays and lesbians, when referring to both sexes.

Chapter Six

Writing Journal Articles

So here is my slightly embarrassed confession—I don't like to write, but I love to have written.

Michael Kanin

Types of Papers

$\mathcal{P}$apers can be either unpublished or published. Unpublished papers include course assignments (e.g., term papers), informal documents (e.g., discussion papers), and preliminary reports (e.g., conference papers). Published papers are formal documents. They are papers that have been specifically prepared for publication. A paper that is packaged (i.e., formatted) for publication is called a manuscript. You submit a manuscript to a publisher, but it is primarily the paper (i.e., the content) that is judged (see Chapter 7). If the paper is rejected, it remains an unpublished manuscript. When it is "unconditionally" accepted, it becomes a published paper. A published paper is one that is either *in press* (to be published) or *in print* (published). Published papers are called articles.

There are two types of scholarly papers: research and conceptual. Research papers are a homogeneous lot. They include descriptive, evaluative, and experimental reports. They must possess three characteristics to qualify:

1. They must be a primary source;
2. They must contain special knowledge; and
3. They must follow a prescribed structure.

The word *primary* means that the material is original; it has not been published elsewhere, in part, or in whole. The term *special* means that the content is discipline-specific; it draws from an established body of research. The word *prescribed* means that the organization is predictable; it conforms to scientific convention. There are four main parts: (a) introduction, (b) method(s), (c) results, and (d) discussion. Combined, they form the acronym IMRAD. IMRAD is the community standard. There are exceptions, but most research-based disciplines subscribe to this format for the writing of either qualitative or quantitative research reports.

Conceptual papers are a heterogeneous lot. They are a blend of facts, observation, opinion, research, and theory. They vary greatly because

1. They may be either a primary or a secondary source;
2. They may contain either general or special knowledge; and
3. They may follow either a prescribed or an innovative structure.

Some are confrontational, some are developmental, and some are philosophical. There are six prototypes:

1. A critique/rebuttal/rejoinder
2. A how-to paper
3. An information paper
4. A literature review
5. A philosophical treatise
6. A position paper.

A critique is a critical assessment of a literary work. The work may be research-based, theory-based, or a combination. The objective is to challenge and provoke debate by illustrating flaws in logic, design, analysis, interpretation, and the like. Flaws in logic could be due to false assumptions, misleading examples, omission of fact, or distortion of fact. Flaws in design could be due to inaccurate sampling, poor operational definition, or weak instrumentation. Flaws in analysis could be due to incorrect classification, incomplete data processing, or inappropriate statistical testing. Flaws in interpretation could be due to biased explanation, unsupported cause-and-effect arguments, or hasty generalization.

The rebuttal, sometimes called the retort, is the defence. The author defends his or her work by advancing counterarguments. Counterarguments may be either systematic or selective. A systematic attack attempts to refute each criticism in the order presented. A selective attack addresses only pertinent points. It is used when critics dwell on insignificant items, overburden the reader with detail, or belabour small errors of fact. Counterarguments vary, but typically begin with a general statement followed by an elaboration. For example, the author may accuse the critic of exaggeration or sensationalism (a general statement). The elaboration contains three steps: (a) identify the text (quote or paraphrase it); (b) note the error; and (c) correct the error. You may reiterate your stance and fortify it with new information.

The rejoinder is the critic's reply to the author. The critic has three options. The first is to persist, the second is to compromise, and the third is to concede. Persistence requires conviction, compromise requires respect, and concession requires humility. A balance is recommended. Throughout, the contestants should avoid *ad hominem*, *ad populum*, and *ad verecundiam* arguments (see Chapter 2).

A how-to paper is a documented account of a professional activity. The author is usually an inquisitive practitioner, someone who initiates and inspires change in their practice. The emphasis is on process or product, or both. The paper, for instance, could be based on a mechanical procedure, a technical operation, or an instructional technique. Data are gathered on-site through participant observation. Journals are used to record field events in naturalistic settings. Reporting is primarily anecdotal. Recommendations centre on proficiency, efficiency, or expediency. The papers often serve as a stimulus for further study.

An information paper is a summation, an abridged version of a topic. The purpose is to disseminate knowledge—to create awareness, appreciation, and understanding. It is written much like a chapter in a college or university textbook. The focus is on content. The coverage is encyclopedic. The six driving forces are what, why, when, how, where, and who. The paper could be a biographical sketch; a historical synopsis; or a descriptive overview of a condition (e.g., a health problem), an object (e.g., a gas turbine), a situation (e.g., a labour strike), or a theory (e.g., Piaget's stages of cognitive development).

ॐॐॐॐ

I keep six honest serving-men

(They taught me all I knew);

Their names are What and Why and When

And How and Where and Who.

Rudyard Kipling

ॐॐॐॐ

A literature review is a systematic survey of selected research in a field. The purpose is to take stock. There are two types: state-of-the-art and meta-analysis (Gall, Gall, & Borg, 2003). The traditional approach is state-of-the-art. It is an interpretative, narrative summary and critique of the literature. A meta-analysis is an "analysis of (the) analyses" (Glass, McGaw, & Smith, 1981, p. 12). It statistically combines the findings of several independently conducted quantitative studies.

> The approach to research integration referred to as "meta-analysis" is nothing more than the attitude of data analysis applied to quantitative summaries of individual experiments. By recording the properties of studies and their findings in quantitative terms, the meta-analysis of research invites one who would integrate numerous and diverse findings to apply the full power of statistical methods to the task. Thus it is not a technique; rather it is a perspective that uses many techniques of measurement and statistical analysis. (p. 21)

The steps are essentially the same for both types of review. First, identify your topic. What is your review question? Does it have subparts? If so, what are they? Second, justify the review. What purpose will it serve? Who will benefit from it? Is it needed? Why? Third, describe your search (see Chapter 3). What databases did you use? What subject headings did you use? What restrictions, if any, did you put on your searches? Did you confine them to specific countries? Did you limit them to specific years? And so on. Fourth, detail your selection process. How did you screen the material? What criteria did you use? What was excluded? What was included? What is the size of your collection? Fifth, describe your analysis. How did you integrate the material? How was it recorded? How was it scored? How was it summarized? State-of-the-art reviews use techniques such as vote-counting. Studies are compiled, coded, and classified according to predetermined categories. A simple classification system might be: positive relationship, negative relationship, no relationship. In contrast, meta-analysis uses multivariate statistical techniques such as factor analysis or multiple regression analysis (Gall et al., 2003; Norman & Streiner, 1997). The findings of all the studies are the dependent variable in the analysis. The independent variables are the studies' substantive (e.g., age of respondents) and methodological (e.g., sample size) characteristics. Sixth, present your findings. Are they consistent? Are they statistically significant? What do they reveal? And seventh, discuss your findings within the parameters of your data set and distinguish between narrative-generated and numerical-generated conclusions.

A philosophical treatise is a reflection paper devoted to theory building or theory refinement, or both. Theory is defined as a set of interrelated ideas (constructs) and hypotheses that specify relationships among variables. The primary purpose of theory is to predict and develop tentative explanations of natural phenomena. It does this by extrapolation. It assesses the past, it clarifies the present, and it predicts the future. The direction is always from the known to the unknown. Predictions are based on systematic observation of the phenomena. When the observations validate the predictions, the theory is accepted. When the observations invalidate the predictions, the theory is rejected. This leads to new theory building which, in turn, is tested, modified, and redefined. The process is cyclical. Theory governs prediction, prediction governs observation, and observation governs theory.

Philosophical papers, then, help summarize facts, explain phenomena, and advance theory.

A position paper, sometimes called an opinion piece, is a calculated commentary on a contemporary, controversial issue. The objective is to take sides, to either support or challenge a plan, policy, practice, principle, or program. There are eight steps:

1. Identify the issue;
2. Place it in its proper context;
3. State your position;
4. Weigh the evidence for;
5. Weigh the evidence against;
6. Compare and contrast 4 and 5;
7. Reaffirm your position; and
8. Close with conviction.

You can compare and contrast 4 and 5 either separately or simultaneously. The evidence "for," however, must be compelling. Critical arguments based on personal experience are less compelling than those based on research. Do not confuse opinion with fact. Do not use false logic. And do not resort to *ad hominem, ad populum,* and *ad verecundiam* arguments (see Chapter 2).

Parts of a Paper

All papers have a beginning, a middle, and an end. The beginning is the introduction, the middle is the body, and the end is the conclusion.

The Introduction

A strong introduction is critical to the success and acceptance of a paper. It normally contains five parts: the lead, the background, the thesis, the rationale, and the summary. The lead is the opening line or paragraph. A good lead has three characteristics. First, it is concrete;

it appeals to the senses. Second, it is natural; it blends into the text. And third, it is effective; it moves the reader. Examples include:

1. An anecdote
2. A challenge
3. A current event
4. A figure of speech
5. A formal definition
6. A forecast or prediction
7. A novel quotation
8. A statistic.

Different papers, different leads. A research paper, for example, might begin with a formal definition or a statistic whereas a conceptual paper might begin with a figure of speech or a forecast.

The background sets the stage. It bridges the gap between your work and that of others. Ideally, it should be limited to two or three secondary sources, preferably review articles.

The thesis gives focus (see Chapter 3). It is the seed from which the paper grows. It is the "promise" to the reader which the author fulfils. The promise can take different forms. For instance, it could be a hypothesis which the writer opposes or defends or it could be a research question which the author answers. "Editors of scholarly journals agree that one of the most common and frustrating problems with submitted articles is a failure on the part of authors to express their thesis clearly and early in the article" (Olson, 1997, p. 59).

ॐॐॐॐ

If your research is strong, then everyone should know it. So state what you did up front—the first paragraph, even the first sentence—and leave the dilly-dallying for people who don't have anything to report.

Erich Kunhardt

ॐॐॐॐ

The rationale justifies your paper. It identifies a weakness in the literature and addresses it. It answers the question: So what? You "must" add to the literature and you must have "good reason" for doing so. Examples include:

1. No recent studies
2. A gap in the research
3. Poor operational definition
4. Confusion in terminology
5. Classification errors
6. Faulty design
7. False assumptions
8. Isolated samples
9. Weak instrumentation
10. Insufficient controls
11. Superficial analysis
12. Contradictory findings
13. Inconclusive results
14. Ambiguous interpretation
15. Inaccurate interpretation
16. Distortion of fact
17. Omission of fact
18. Overgeneralization
19. Impressionistic views
20. Incomplete, misleading, or weak documentation.

The above items are not necessarily exclusive. In fact, one often leads to another. Hence, you could have more than one rationale. The point is, you need a sound reason for writing your paper and you must state it at the outset. The amount of space devoted to this task

> depends on your audience. If your readers are experts in your field, you may not have to justify your work explicitly—your readers might implicitly understand the importance. However, not justifying your work limits your audience. (Alley, 1996, p. 30)

The summary gives the reader a quick preview of the paper. It maps the structure and lists the subtopics. The order once established must be followed.

The Body

The body is the largest part of the paper. It contains information (data, definitions, examples, facts, theory, etc.) that develops the main ideas of your thesis. The structure of conceptual papers depends on the order of development and the level of subordination (see Chapter 3). The former gives direction to your writing, the latter gives depth to your writing. Together, they determine the type of writing (see Chapter 2). A how-to paper, for example, might use two orders of development (increasing complexity & cause and effect), five levels of subordination (I., II.; I. A., I. B.; I. A. 1., I. A. 2; I. A. 1. a., I. A. 1. b.; I. A. 1. b. i, I. A. 1. b. ii), and two types of writing (description & exposition). See Figure 6-1 for other possible combinations.

Research papers follow a standard structure. Most contain the following sections and subsections:

    A. Literature Review

    B. Method(s)

        1. Instrumentation or Materials

        2. Data Collection or Sampling Procedure

        3. Data Analysis

    C. Results or Findings.

The Method section and the Results section are always part of the body. The literature review, though, may be part of the body or part of the background section in the introduction.

A. Literature Review

The literature review assesses the strengths and limitations of previous investigations. It examines important methodological issues, significant findings, and major conclusions.

Type of Paper	Order of Development	Type of Writing
1. A critique/ rebuttal/ rejoinder	Increasing importance/ general to particular/ particular to general/ cause & effect/ comparison & contrast	Argumentation/description/ exposition
2. A how-to paper	Space/increasing complexity/ cause & effect	Description/exposition
3. An information paper	Space/object/increasing complexity/increasing importance/decreasing importance/cause & effect/ comparison & contrast	Description/exposition/ narration
4. A literature review	Time/increasing importance/ decreasing importance/ particular to general/ comparison & contrast	Description/exposition/ narration
5. A philosophical treatise	Time/general to particular/ particular to general/ cause & effect	Description/exposition/ narration
6. A position paper	Increasing importance/ general to particular/ particular to general/ cause & effect/ comparison & contrast	Argumentation/description/ exposition

Figure 6-1. Structural combinations for conceptual papers.

Often the review is organized in either time order or space order (see Chapter 3). Time order is from the distant past to the most recent. You might, for example, divide a review into three periods: The Early Years (1970–1989), The Middle Years (1990–1999), and The Recent Years (2000–present).

Space order is from one location to another. You might, for instance, divide a review into Canada's five regions starting in the west and moving to the east (British Columbia, the Prairie Provinces, Ontario, Quebec, the Maritime Provinces). Or, you might move from far to near (Europe, United States, Canada, Alberta, Edmonton). Sometimes the two orders are combined.

B. Method

The Method section describes the research design. It tells the reader what you did and how you did it. You must give enough information to permit replication. The section is normally divided into three subsections: instrumentation, data collection, and data analysis.

1. Instrumentation

This subsection describes the equipment, the materials, and the measurement devices used to gather information. How many instruments did you use? Which instruments did you use? Check as many as apply:

interview schedules	_____
inventories	_____
questionnaires	_____
tests	_____
other (specify)	_____ _____

Did you borrow an instrument? Did you create an instrument? Acknowledge those you borrow. Describe those you create. What do they measure? Are they valid? Are they reliable? What is the item format? What is the response mode? Give examples.

2. Data Collection

This subsection provides information on the study locale, the sample, and the administration or treatment. Give the location of the study. Where were the data collected? How were they collected? Describe the procedures. Paraphrase the instructions. Who participated? How many participated? How were they selected? Was it a random sample? Was it a convenience sample? How many were in the control group? How many were in the experimental group? Describe the demographics. How many were males? How many were females? How many were high school graduates? How many were university graduates? And so on.

3. Data Analysis

This subsection describes how the data were processed. How were the data recorded? How were they scored? How were they tabulated? How were they analyzed? Did you use descriptive statistics, or inferential statistics, or both (Babbie, 2001; Elmes et al., 2003; Gall et al., 2003)? Did you use an analysis of variance (ANOVA) (Huck & Cormier, 1996; Jackson, 1999; Norman & Streiner, 1997)? If so, acknowledge the program used, describe how it was used, but do not try to justify its use (e.g., ANOVAs were computed between means using the Statistical Package for the Social Sciences Version 14.0 [SPSS Version 14.0]).

C. Results

This section begins with a restatement of your research question(s). State the main findings, including those that are controversial or unexpected. Figures and tables are often used to accent your results (see Chapter 4). They should be identified in text before they are presented (e.g., Table 1 indicates...; (see Figure 2); As shown in Table 3,....). Include all pertinent information such as test values (t values, F values, etc.), degrees of freedom (df), levels of probability ($p < .01$, etc.), and effect size (ES = .20, .50, .80) (Cohen, 1988).

The Conclusion

The conclusion brings closure to a topic. Like the body, it is divided into different sections and subsections depending on the type of paper you write. A research report is normally divided into three sections: summary statement, discussion, and recommendations or implications. The summary answers three questions:

1. What did you do?
2. How did you do it?
3. What did you find?

The discussion puts your findings in perspective. It notes similarities and differences between your results and the literature and it offers an interpretation. The recommendations can be theoretical (construct-oriented), practical (action-oriented), empirical (research-oriented), or all three. Theoretical implications must be related to the construct or model on which your work was based. You might challenge some of the basic principles, offer alternatives, or propose changes. Practical suggestions are field-based. They too must evolve from your findings. You might, for instance, indicate how a particular finding could benefit an association, an institution, or society-at-large. Recommendations for further research are tied to the limitations of your inquiry. You might, for example, suggest that more studies be conducted using larger samples, refined instrumentation, or additional controls.

Conceptual types vary, but most contain a summary statement and a discussion section. The summary answers three questions:

1. What was your purpose?
2. How did you achieve it?
3. What did you conclude?

The discussion puts your summary in perspective. It could assess the present situation in relation to past developments or it could speculate on future developments, be they short- or long-term, or both. Sometimes, the discussion is followed by a concluding statement in which the reader is pressed to take stock, to reevaluate, and to act.

Revising the Text

Writing and revising are distinct activities. Each requires a different mindset. Writing is creating, revising is criticizing. Do not mix the two as they

> interfere with each other: first write freely and uncritically so that you can generate as many words and ideas as possible without worrying whether they are good; then turn around and adopt a critical frame of mind and thoroughly revise what you have written—taking what's good and discarding what isn't and shaping what's left into something strong. (Elbow, 1998, p. 7)

Revising, like writing, is hard work. There are no shortcuts. It requires a "certain ruthlessness" (p. 33). You must step outside yourself, become detached, and

> learn the pleasures of the knife. Learn to retreat, to cut your losses, to be chicken. Learn to say, "Yes, I *care* more about this passage than about any other, I'm involved in it, but for that very reason, I can't make it work right. Out it goes!" (p. 37)

You may have struggled for hours or days over a section, then suddenly realize that it is redundant. At first, you deny it; then, you confront it. You try to save part of it, but to no avail. You try to rearrange it, but to no avail. It haunts you. It corners you. It breaks you. It feels like you are cutting off a finger, but you will endure.

෨෨෧෧

A writer is unfair to himself when he is unable to be hard on himself.

Marianne Moore

෨෨෧෧

Revising is a skill. And like any other skill, the development of skill excellence takes practice, patience, and perseverance. The following seven steps will help. First, set your paper aside for a week. Let it cool. The interval will give you fresh insights. Second, pretend that someone else wrote your paper.

> Since it is often easier to see faults in the work of others than in your own, pretend that you are revising someone else's draft. If you can look at your writing and ask, "How could *he* or *she* have written that?" you are in the right frame of mind to revise. (Oliu et al., 1994, p. 82)

Third, establish a system. You have two choices. You can revise from detail to part to whole or from whole to part to detail. Fourth, make successive passes through your manuscript, checking for one component at a time. For instance, you might start with the content, move to the structure, and then to the craft. Fifth, keep your sessions short: 60 to 90 minutes. When you stop cutting, take a break. Sixth, keep a list of your most common errors (double-check them). And seventh, remember

> whenever you revise the manuscript, you tend to create still other inconsistencies. As you add or delete figures, tables, equations, references, and footnotes, you disturb the numbering system. These changes must be checked carefully so that, for example, a new chart numbered "Figure 6" will match your explanation of Figure 6 in the text. (Michaelson, 1990, p. 120)

Revision is tedious work, but it is rewarding. It reinforces your image as writer. It gives you a deep sense of accomplishment. It gives "you" pride in product. It gives "you" pride in self.

Revisions can be done on the computer or on a hard copy, or both. Hard copy is recommended because flaws are spotted more easily on a printed page. Once identified, the revisions can be entered into the electronic document. Number and save all drafts under different file names so that they can be easily identified and retrieved if you decide later to merge parts from them.

Below is a series of checklists. They are organized from whole to part to detail. You can use this approach, or one with which you feel comfortable. The order of your passes is not important. What is important is that you be systematic, objective, and thorough. Go slowly. Scan, read, reflect, revise, reread. Scan, read, reflect, revise, reread, and so on.

A. Check your Content:

1. Is there one central idea around which everything evolves?
2. Does everything have a purpose? State it!
3. Is your material correct (facts, formulas, numbers, quotations, etc.)?
4. Is the text well-documented?
5. Are your sources bona fide?
6. Are they up-to-date?
7. Is there missing information?
8. Is there irrelevant information?
9. Is there contradiction?
10. Is there distortion?
11. Is there duplication?
12. Is there overgeneralization?

B. Check your Structure:

1. Organization

   a. Is the text well-organized?
   b. What is (are) your order(s) of development?
   c. Is there a clearly defined beginning, middle, and end?
   d. Is there a balanced relationship among the parts?
   e. Do the parts make a whole?
   f. Are there unnecessary digressions?
   g. Is everything in place?

2. Paragraphs

   a. Is the first paragraph interesting?
   b. Does it set the stage for what is to follow?
   c. Is each paragraph founded on a topic sentence?
   d. Does each paragraph have a oneness about it?

     e. Do they vary in length?
     f. Are there too many short, underdeveloped paragraphs?
     g. Are there too many long, convoluted paragraphs?
     h. Is each paragraph developed logically?
     i. Is each sequenced properly?
     j. Is there interconnectedness between paragraphs?
     k. Are the interconnections (transitions) smooth?
     l. Does the last paragraph give a sense of completion?

3. Sentences

     a. Are there incomplete sentences?
     b. Are there run-on sentences?
     c. Is there a variety of sentence structure (simple, complex, compound, compound-complex)?
     d. Is there continuity of thought from sentence to sentence?
     e. Are there too many sentences?

C. Check your Craft:

1. Do your words convey the meaning intended?
2. Are they stated in terms the reader can understand?
3. Do you limit big words (polysyllables)?
4. Do you limit jargon (wordese)?
5. Do you avoid tautologies (redundancies)?
6. Do you avoid circumlocution (roundabout expressions)?
7. Do you limit euphemisms (inexact expressions)?
8. Do you limit clichés (stale expressions)?
9. Do you avoid discriminatory language (biased expressions)?

10. Do you avoid colloquialisms (informal expressions)?
11. Do you limit neologisms (newly coined expressions)?
12. Do you limit qualifiers?
13. Do you use a variety of transitions?
14. Do you use parallel structures?
15. Do you define your terms?
16. Do you give examples?
17. Do you avoid rehashes (echo)?

Editing the Text

You edit to ensure correct copy. It is the final, word-by-word, line-by-line, section-by-section check on grammar, spelling, word usage, and format.

Editing should be done in two stages. First, edit onscreen, and second, edit a hard copy. You will often spot errors on the hard copy that you missed onscreen. Word-processing programs have editing features that will help you check grammar, spelling, and formatting. Although, initially, they may be helpful, ultimately, you will have to run manual checks on your grammar and spelling because the programs are limited. They can check for errors in subject-verb agreement, for errors in punctuation, for wordiness, and for the reliance on passive constructions, but they cannot judge the context in which a word or phrase is used.

Spell-checkers will catch most spelling errors, but will miss mistakes in word usage (e.g., canon/cannon). In addition, they will miss word processing errors such as the omission or insertion of letters (e.g., bit/bite), the use of wrong letters (e.g., referred/refereed), and letter reversals (e.g., form/from).

Manual checks should focus on one or two items at a time. Make at least three passes through your work. First, check for grammatical errors; second, check for spelling and word usage errors; and third, check for faulty format. Go slowly. Read, edit, reread; read, edit, reread; and so forth. Keep your sessions short: 60 to 90 minutes. Do not over-edit. Quibbling over periods and semicolons, for example, is a waste of time.

఼఼఼఼

Do not be afraid of the semicolon; it can be most useful.

Ernest Gowers

఼఼఼఼

A. Check your Grammar:

    1. Do you overuse the active or passive voice?
    2. Do you avoid sudden shifts in mood, number, person, tense, and voice?
    3. Do you avoid noun-forming suffixes?
    4. Do you limit verb-forming suffixes?
    5. Do you omit misplaced modifiers?
    6. Do you omit dangling modifiers?
    7. Do you omit squinting modifiers?
    8. Do you omit noun strings?
    9. Do you omit double negatives?
    10. Do you omit incomplete comparisons?

B. Check your Spelling:

    1. Is your spelling consistent (see Chapter 4)?
    2. Is your spelling correct? Appendix J contains a list of 100 commonly misspelled words and their corrections. A tailor-made list will help you spot errors.

C. Check your Word Usage:

Is it course or coarse? Is it current or currant? Words that sound the same or alike, but differ in spelling and meaning are called homonyms. Spell-checkers will not detect the incorrect use of homonyms. You will have to run a manual check on the usage of these words. Appendix K contains a list of 50 homonyms. It is not an exhaustive list, but it contains some of the more confusing sets.

D. Check your Format:

1. Is your use of abbreviations consistent throughout?
2. Is your use of capitalization and punctuation consistent throughout?
3. Is your use of headings and subheadings consistent throughout?
4. Do all your illustrations have headings?
5. Are all your illustrations numbered correctly?
6. Are all your textual references to illustrations numbered correctly?
7. Are all your illustrations mentioned in text "before" they appear?
8. Are all handwritten and typewritten words that are to be printed in italics underlined?
9. Do your citations in text correspond with those in your reference list and vice versa?
10. Are there missing references?
11. Is your text double-spaced throughout?
12. Do you use 8 ½ X 11 in. (21.5 X 28 cm) white, bond paper?
13. Are your pages numbered consecutively?
14. Are your pages numbered correctly?
15. Is your running head correct?
16. Are your margins correct (1 in. [2.5 cm] at top, bottom, and sides)?
17. Are your copies clean (no arrows, blots, erasures, inserts)?
18. Are your copies legible?

Writing the Abstract

The abstract appears first, but is written last. It is a 75 to 150 word summary of the introduction, the body, and the conclusion. It should carry the title ABSTRACT or Abstract, be double-spaced, and be typed on a separate page (see Figure 6-2). If the work is the second of a two-part series, note this, cite the source, and give the full bibliographical citation in the reference list. Exclude all other references, paraphrase rather than quote, and avoid abbreviations.

ABSTRACT

This article looks at authorship patterns in CJNR from 1970 to 1991. A tally was taken of the number of single, double and multiple authorships for each year which, in turn, were combined into one seven year and three five year intervals. Frequency counts were converted into percentages, chi-squares were computed, and author/article ratios were calculated for each year. Results revealed a decrease in the number of single authored articles and an increase in the number of co- and multiple authored articles from 1982 on. The author/article ratios fluctuated somewhat, but, overall showed marked increases. It was tentatively concluded that nursing is not unlike other disciplines, that it too is experiencing changes in authorship patterns. Reasons for the changes are tendered along with suggestions for further research. (Norris, 1993, p. 151)

Figure 6-2. An example of an abstract.

Abstracts test your writing. A good one is succinct; a poor one is verbose. A good one will hold readers; a poor one will lose readers. Like the summary in your conclusion, an abstract answers three questions. For research papers,

1. What did you do?
2. How did you do it?
3. What did you find?

For conceptual papers,

1. What was your purpose?
2. How did you achieve it?
3. What did you conclude?

Finding a Title

A good title is inclusive, informative, and interesting. It compresses the substance of your paper into as few words as possible. Like abstracts, titles give first impressions. And since titles appear only on content pages and in most indexes, often they alone are instrumental in deciding whether an article will be read or passed by.

❯❯❮❮

The Ancient Mariner would not have taken so well if it had been called The Old Sailor.

Samuel Butler

❯❯❮❮

You can write titles at any time, but you should revisit them when you finish your abstract. Start by brainstorming. Write down three or four titles, including your earlier versions. See which words appear in most of them. Then ask yourself: What words would catch my attention if I saw them in a table of contents or an index? These are your keywords. Next, play around with the order. Place keywords at the beginning, in the middle, and at the end. Avoid abbreviations and capitalize all words except

1. Articles (a, an, the),
2. Conjunctions with fewer than four letters,
3. Prepositions with fewer than four letters.

You can use the exclamation mark and the question mark, but never end a title with a period even if it is a complete sentence. If your title has two lines, make the second shorter than the first.

Sometimes two-part titles are more effective than single ones. The two parts are separated by a colon, the first part being a general statement, the second a specific statement. Examples include:

Publish or Perish: Dispelling the Myth
Politics or Perish: Confirming the Myth

Giving Acknowledgements

Acknowledgements are reserved for those who made contributions that do not qualify for authorship (see Chapter 9). There are four types. First, acknowledge editorial assistance provided by copy editors and proofreaders. Second, acknowledge those who made procedural contributions. Included are those who conducted literature searches (e.g., reference librarians), those who arranged for participants (e.g., associates, colleagues, friends), those who collected data (e.g., graduate students, research assistants), and those who provided office space and equipment (e.g., chairpersons, deans, directors). Third, acknowledge those who made technical contributions. Included are statistical consultants, computer programmers, and word processors. And fourth, acknowledge financial aid provided by local, national, and international granting agencies. As a rule, you acknowledge "only" support staff who made specific contributions above and beyond their "normal" call of duty (King, McGuire, Longman, & Carroll-Johnson, 1997, p. 164).

It is best to get written permission from the individual, group, or institution that you are acknowledging. You should show them the "exact" wording as they

> might well believe that your acknowledgement is insufficient or (worse) that it is too effusive....An inappropriate thank you can be worse than none at all, and if you value the advice and help of friends and colleagues, you should be careful to thank them in a way that pleases rather than displeases them. (Day, 1998, p. 50)

The credit is usually given in a footnote below the last line of text on the first page or in an endnote between the last line of text and the reference list on the last page. A superscript, normally an Arabic number, is used with the footnote. It is placed at the end of the title and at the beginning of the credit. The subtitle Acknowledgement(s) or Note(s) is used with the endnote. Examples include:

1. The author thanks Dr. Nancy Latimer for helpful suggestions on organization and presentation of this paper.
2. The authors thank Dr. Kathleen Gates for helping to

research material for this article.
3.   The author is indebted to Paul N. Sachis for his assistance with the data analysis.
4.   The authors thank Anne Balon for formatting the final version of this manuscript.
5.   This publication was supported in part by a research grant from the Faculty of Medicine, Canuck University.

Chapter Seven

Getting Published

A publisher is somebody looking for someone who has something to say.

Lorne Pierce

Locating Outlets

γou should locate two or three potential outlets for your article before you write it. These are known as your target journals. If you cannot find at least two, drop, reduce, or expand your topic. There is no point in writing a paper that has no chance of getting published.

If you are undecided or cannot find a satisfactory outlet, check Appendix A or one of the periodical directories in Appendix H. Appendix A contains a list of 420 Canadian periodicals in 50 categories. Appendix H contains five periodical directories:

1. *Directory of Scholarly Electronic Journals and Academic Discussion Lists,*
2. *Gale Directory of Publications and Broadcast Media,*
3. *MLA Directory of Periodicals,*
4. *Standard Periodical Directory,* and
5. *Ulrich's Periodicals Directory.*

Make a list of your most promising outlets. Some may be print journals, others may be electronic journals, and still others may be in both print and electronic media. A print journal is a bound, hard copy edition.

An electronic journal, sometimes called an on-line journal, is

> a genuine academic journal that is published and disseminated primarily via electronic media....Some of the journals are peer reviewed just like their paper counterparts. They cover a wide range of topics, ranging from fine art to issues concerning the handicapped [*sic*], to library science and ethnomusicology. (Ressler, 1997, pp. 311–312)

Divide your list into electronic journals and print journals. Look for the Author Information page. The title may vary. For example, it is sometimes called the Manuscript Information page, the Instructions to Authors page, the Notes for Authors page, and the like. Visit the home page of each electronic journal and check its navigation bar. Click on links that may give you the information you seek. If you cannot find the information, check the print copy. If there is no print copy, e-mail the editor.

Print copies may be located in your library. Check the on-line catalogue for its latest list of holdings. If there are no recent issues, request a copy of the Author Information page through interlibrary loan services. If the journal is listed, check the latest issue. The information is usually found at the back, on the last page (the verso) or on the inside of the back cover (the recto), or both. If you cannot find the instructions, check the first issue of the latest volume. Some journals print their guidelines only once a year, in the first issue of each volume.

Never submit a manuscript to a journal without first having studied the Author Information page. A typical Author Information page is shown in Figure 7-1. It contains (a) the editorial policy, (b) the manuscript guidelines, (c) the subscription rates, and (d) the citations list. The editorial policy presents information on frequency of publication (the number of issues per year), the type of material sought (content), the author's responsibilities (accuracy, credits, permissions), and the review process (nonrefereed or refereed).

The manuscript guidelines provide directions on style and format, submission, and deposition. Style and format deal with the technical aspects of the manuscript. Included are requirements on the length, typing, and presentation of illustrations. Submission includes information on the number of copies to be submitted, preparation of the title page, computer requirements, and postage. Deposition includes information on acknowledgements; the time intervals between receipt, review, and possible acceptance or rejection; copyright; complimentary copies; and reprints.

Subscription rates for different subscribers, as well as for back issues, are given in the currency of the host country unless stated otherwise.

The citations list indicates in which periodical indexes or abstract indexes, or both, the articles are listed.

TITLE: The Canadian Journal of Research (CJR) [fictitious]

ADDRESS: Canuck University [fictitious]
000 University Avenue South
Ottawa, ON
Canada X1Y 2Z3

SPONSORSHIP: The Canadian Research Association (CRA) [fictitious]

EDITORIAL POLICY

Issues: Quarterly

Content: The *Journal* publishes articles that employ applied research methods. Both qualitative and quantitative pieces are sought. Potential contributors are encouraged to submit case studies, content analyses studies, correlational studies, descriptive studies, experimental studies, historical studies, and reports on measuring the effectiveness of innovative programs.

Responsibility: The author bears full responsibility for accurately listing quotations, crediting sources, and obtaining permission to quote lengthy excerpts from previously published material. The views expressed are the sole responsibility of the individual authors; neither the *Journal* nor its editors and reviewers assume responsibility for the statements or opinions expressed by contributors.

Review Process: Refereed

MANUSCRIPT (ms.) GUIDELINES

Style and Format: APA (5th ed., 2001). Preferred length 3,000-5,000 words; 10-20 pages, typewritten, double-spaced including references on one side of 8.5" x 11" paper with ample margins justified left; abstract of 75-150 words. All figures and tables must be presented on separate pages, camera-ready. The position of each should be clearly marked in the text with the phrase

(Insert Figure 1 about here) or (Insert Table 1 about here). There is a limit of 3 illustrations per ms.

Submission: Enclose 3 copies. Simultaneous submission not permitted. Separate title page with date submitted, ms. title, author's name, address and institutional affiliation, phone and fax numbers, and e-mail address required. Ms. **not** to contain the author's name. Include a self-addressed, stamped envelope for the return of unaccepted ms. Submit accepted ms. on a diskette or CD-ROM using IBM-compatible word processing programs such as WordPerfect or Microsoft Word.

Disposition: Receipt of ms. is acknowledged. All correspondence directed to first author if more than one author. Decision in 6 months. Published 6 to 8 months after acceptance. Rejected ms. is returned with comments. Copyright held by the *Journal*. Authors are granted permission to reproduce copies of their work within an issue. Each author receives two complimentary copies of the issue in which their article appears. Reprints available at cost.

Send to: P. J. Jones, Editor

SUBSCRIPTION

Annual Rate(s): $80.00 (Cdn.) for institutions, $50.00 (Cdn.) for individuals, $30.00 (Cdn.) for students, domestic and foreign. Please add $8.00 (Cdn.) per year for delivery outside Canada. CRA membership: $140.00 (Cdn.) includes four annual issues. Single and back issue copies are $20.00 each. Make cheques payable to *The Canadian Journal of Research*.

Inquiries: Address as above.

CITATIONS   CINAHL (Cumulative Index to Nursing and Allied Health Literature), ERIC (Educational Resources Information Centre), Science Citation Index, Social Science Citation Index; appropriate articles are abstracted in Psychological Abstracts, and Research into Higher Education Abstracts.

Figure 7-1. A typical Author Information page.

How do you select a journal? There are so many. Some are subject-specific, others are mixed. Some publish only research-based articles, some publish only theory-based articles, and some publish both. Some have an international focus, some have a national focus, and some, especially in the United States, are state-focused. Some are sponsored by commercial presses, some are sponsored by learned societies, and some are sponsored by institutions. Some have only theme issues, others have no theme issues, and still others have both theme and nontheme issues. Some administer internal reviews, some conduct external reviews, and some do both. Some use two reviewers, others use three reviewers, and still others use five or more reviewers.

So, how do you decide? There are at least four factors to consider. First, is match. Mismatches have been reported as the single greatest reason for rejection of manuscripts (Day, 1996). A paper could be novel, well-researched, and soundly written, but unacceptable because the authors failed to do their homework. You must read and reread the Author Information page of each target journal. What sort of material is it looking for? Does the journal have a niche? If so, what is it? Spend a morning looking at back issues. Check their contents; look at their writing styles, layouts, graphics, and references. Become familiar with your target journals.

Second, is visibility. Visibility is gained through exposure. And exposure is gained through the periodical indexes and the abstract indexes. If there is no exposure, your readership will be confined to subscribers and their friends. Therefore, it is best to publish in journals that are listed in several of the indexes. Remember,

> as an author, you are interested in maximizing the amount of coverage your article receives. My bottom-line recommendation is that you opt to send your manuscripts to journals abstracted by one or more of the major abstracting services, in lieu of sending them to journals that are not so abstracted. Generally speaking, abstracting services do not include a journal for review until it is well established, and those that lack such abstracting features can be said to be less credible than those that do not....As in the case of abstracting services, an author should consider whether a given journal is reviewed by the citation index relevant to his or her field. This is perhaps most important for academic authors seeking promotion or tenure. (Thyer, 1994, pp. 20–21, 23)

Third, is scope. Scope is the range of circulation. Some journals have an international scope, others have a national scope, and still others have a provincial scope. Those with an international scope have a wider circulation, but not necessarily a greater circulation, than those with a national or provincial scope. As a rule, though, the range of the circulation is more important than its size. In short, there is more prestige in international publications than in national or provincial publications assuming, of course, that they are of equal or similar quality.

Fourth, is quality. Quality is largely determined by the review process. Basically, there are two types of reviews: *nonrefereed* and *refereed*. In the first case, editors alone decide what will, or will not, be published. They may consult with an editorial board depending on the complexity and diversity of the manuscripts received, but they are not required to do so nor are they bound by the feedback. Consultation is open. It is open because the reviewers know the authors, their credentials, and their academic affiliations. These types of publications are called "nonrefereed."

In the second case, editors screen incoming manuscripts, but the decision to publish depends on reviews conducted by a panel of peers. The reviews are closed because they are anonymous (blind) and independent. Anonymous means that only the title of the manuscript appears on the first page of the paper; the author's name, position, and employment are withheld by the editor. Independent means that the reviewers do not correspond with each other. Rather, they send their evaluations to the editor who, in turn, weighs the feedback and then decides whether a piece will be accepted as is, accepted with minor revisions, accepted with major revisions, or rejected. These types of publications are called "refereed." Refereed publications normally carry more weight in promotion and tenure decisions than nonrefereed publications (Day, 1996; Luey, 2002; O'Neill & Sachis, 1994, 1998; Thyer, 1994). Indeed,

> refereed journals are the bastions of quality in a given field. They have set themselves up to select only those articles which meet the journal's objectives and the standards within the field. The standards are not set by the journal alone; they reflect standards within the community that the journal serves. (Day, 1996, p. 52)

Increasing the Odds

You can increase your chances of getting published by writing for theme issues. Experienced writers will sometimes keep notes on journals that publish only theme issues or the occasional theme issue. They do this because the acceptance rate, on average, is higher for theme issues than for nontheme issues (Henson, 1999). Moreover, by keeping notes, they know what has just been published. They then deliberately avoid these outlets, knowing that most journals will not accept submissions after having carried a theme issue on the topic.

Another way to increase your chances of getting published is to volunteer a chapter for an upcoming book of readings or to volunteer book reviews for journals, or both. As well, belonging to the right associations and meeting the right people can result in invitations to contribute to conferences in which the proceedings are published.

Writing Query Letters

Query letters can save time. For instance, a certain topic may be inappropriate for a given journal or the journal may have just published, or be about to publish, a similar paper. In addition, you may get some free advice. Some editors will suggest changes to your proposed manuscript or suggest alternative outlets, or both.

Not all editors, however, welcome query letters. So how do you decide? The answer is found in the type of manuscript being prepared. Specifically, most theory-based journals welcome query letters; most research-based journals do not.

The letter should be carefully crafted because it is a reflection of your writing skills. It

> should be short and succinct, rarely more than one page. It should inform the editor of the thesis and conclusions of your essay, give a brief rationale as to its contribution to ongoing scholarship, and should briefly mention your professional credentials. (Olson, 1997, p. 58)

The following suggestions will help you structure the text:

1. Begin with an interesting lead.
2. Identify your topic.
3. State your purpose.

   ❖ Are you going to add something new?
   ❖ Are you going to clarify something old?

4. Tell why the readership will be interested.

   ❖ Do you offer practical ideas?
   ❖ Do you offer theoretical insights?
   ❖ Do you offer both?

5. Accent your qualifications.

   ❖ What are your areas of expertise?
   ❖ Have you written in the area before?
   ❖ Enclose examples (tear sheets) of your work.

6. Note your familiarity with the journal.

   ❖ Are you a member of the sponsoring society (if one)?
   ❖ How long have you been a member?
   ❖ Do you subscribe to the journal?
   ❖ Do you read the articles? Give an example. Note how it influenced your thinking.

7. Discuss technical aspects.

   ❖ What approach will you take?
   ❖ How long will the article be?
   ❖ Will there be illustrations? How many?
   ❖ When will the manuscript be ready?

Always use the exact name of the editor, or person to whom you are sending a letter. Never use Dear Sir or Madam. Enclose a return, self-addressed, stamped envelope (SASE) and keep a copy of the letter in your files. Use International Reply Coupons for return postage if you are sending your letters abroad. They can be purchased at Canada Post outlets.

Most editors will respond within 2 to 4 weeks. However, do not expect a promise to publish, especially if you are an unknown author or the journal is refereed. The editor, though,

> may enthusiastically encourage you to submit your article, or may suggest that what you are working on is not quite appropriate for the journal's publication schedule at this time, thereby saving you many wasted months in the review process. (p. 58)

Preparing Submissions

Submit your manuscript to your first-choice target journal. If you are undecided, talk to established writers. Ask them: Which one is the best? How do they know? What features do you look for? Then, ask yourself: Where do I want to be in 10 years? If you aspire to national or international stature, your work must be accepted in national and international circles. Simply put, you cannot gain status in a particular community of scholars unless your work is screened and endorsed by that community. Members

> are measured primarily not by their dexterity in laboratory manipulations, not by their innate knowledge of either broad or narrow scientific subjects, and certainly not by their wit or charm; they are measured, and become known (or remain unknown) by their publications. (Day, 1998, p. ix)

It is like a "rite of passage" where individuals are judged by their work, not by their associations, rank, or title. Acceptance implies endorsement through peer review.

Thus, as a rule, you should avoid professional magazines and trade journals that take the position "let a thousand thistles bloom." Remember, print is permanent. Once in print, each publication becomes a measure of your scholarship. Therefore, a poor or weak publication is often worse than no publication at all. Indeed,

> a paper published in a "garbage" journal simply does not equal a paper published in a prestigious journal. In fact, the wise old bird (and there are quite a few around in science) may be more impressed by the candidate with one or two solid publications in a prestigious

journal than by the candidate with 10 or more publications in second-rate journals. (Day, 1998, p. 111)

❧❧❧❧

A hundred cents of copper, though they make more clatter and fill more space, have only a tenth of the value of one eagle of gold.

Emma Hart Willard

❧❧❧❧

Never submit the same manuscript to more than one journal at a time. It is unethical to do so (see Chapter 9). In fact, some journals will require the author to state, or sign a statement to the effect, that the work has not already been published, is not now in press or under consideration elsewhere, and will not be submitted elsewhere while under review.

Each submission should be accompanied by a cover letter (see Figure 7-2) and a separate title or cover page (see Figure 7-3). Keep your letter businesslike. Do not resort to flattery or pressure tactics. Do not say things like "everyone says that your journal is the best in its field," even though it might be. Or, "please hurry the review as other journals have expressed an interest in my work." Silly comments like these could harm the review.

> In corresponding with the editor, keep your letter short; there is no need for a lengthy persuasive rationale for accepting your article. In fact, your letter of transmittal should be brief, simply requesting that the editor consider your article for publication. Unless there is some kind of unusual circumstance that needs to be noted, there is no need to outline your article or discuss its thesis. The article should stand on its own merit. (Olson, 1997, pp. 63–64)

The body of the letter should contain two short working paragraphs. The first paragraph should state the purpose of your correspondence. The second should list your enclosures, confirm compliance with the conditions of the review, and ask for an acknowledgement. End by thanking the editor.

The title page should include the title of your manuscript, the "exact" name by which you wish to be published, your affiliation, your interests, and the date submitted.

November 28, 2005

P. J. Jones, Editor
Canadian Journal of Research
Canuck University
000 University Avenue South
Ottawa, ON X1Y 2Z3

Dear P. J. Jones:

I would like to submit the enclosed manuscript entitled "In Defence of the Doctoral Dissertation" to the *Canadian Journal of Research* for publication.

I have enclosed a title page, three (3) copies of the manuscript, and a self-addressed, stamped envelope. The first copy contains the full text. The remaining copies have self-references masked. The piece has not already been published, is not now in press, or under consideration elsewhere. An acknowledgement would be appreciated.

I thank you for your consideration.

Yours truly,

G. Patrick O'Neill, Ph.D.

Encls.

Figure 7-2. An example of a cover letter.

TITLE:	In Defence of the Doctoral Dissertation
AUTHOR:	G. Patrick O'Neill
AFFILIATION:	Professor of Education, Graduate Department, Faculty of Education, Brock University, St. Catharines, ON CANADA L2S 3A1
INTERESTS:	Higher education, scholarly writing, teacher education, teacher evaluation
DATE SUBMITTED:	November 28, 2005

Figure 7-3. A typical title page.

Submit everything required, including the correct number of copies, a proper disk, and an acknowledgement-of-receipt, self-addressed, stamped envelope. Use an International Reply Coupon for return postage if you are sending your manuscript abroad. Send your package by courier. Use a padded envelope, seal the ends, record the date, and keep a copy of everything for your files.

Seeking an Acknowledgement

On average, you can expect a confirmation of receipt within 2 to 4 weeks. However, there are many exceptions to this rule depending on (a) the editor's timetable, (b) the mail service, and (c) the backlog of manuscripts. If you do not receive an acknowledgement within 4 weeks, send the editor a follow-up letter like the one illustrated in Figure 7-4.

The first follow-up letter is identical, in many respects, to the original cover letter. Added features include an orientation and some speculation as to why an acknowledgement was not received. The orientation should contain the first submission date, the title of the article, and the journal to which it was submitted. The speculation should centre on why an acknowledgement was not received. Here, tact is of utmost importance. Blame should be directed toward an outside agency, not the editor. For example, do not say, "I was wondering if my manuscript was lost or misplaced." The immediate response is "lost or misplaced" by whom? To imply that the editor is incompetent or remiss is not diplomatic even though, occasionally, this will be the reason for the delay.

January 7, 2006

P. J. Jones, Editor
Canadian Journal of Research
Canuck University
000 University Avenue South
Ottawa, ON X1Y 2Z3

Dear P. J. Jones:

On November 28, 2005, I submitted a manuscript entitled "In Defence of the Doctoral Dissertation" to the *Canadian Journal of Research*. Since I have not received an acknowledgement, I was wondering if the materials have been lost, or delayed, in transit. Assuming this to be the case, I am enclosing another title page, three (3) more copies of my manuscript, and an additional self-addressed, stamped envelope.

Once again, I thank you for your consideration.

Yours truly,

G. Patrick O'Neill, Ph.D.

Encls.

Figure 7-4. An example of a first follow-up letter.

If you do not get a reply within 2 weeks, send a second follow-up letter similar to the one shown in either Figure 7-5 or 7-6. At this stage you can safely assume that the manuscript has been received. Hence, there is no need for additional enclosures. However, before proceeding, ask yourself a crucial question: Can I afford to lose more time or should I bring closure? If time is on your side, draft a letter like that illustrated in Figure 7-5. If time is not on your side, bring closure as suggested in Figure 7-6. In either case, you should request an "immediate" response because the material is aging.

January 25, 2006

P. J. Jones, Editor
Canadian Journal of Research
Canuck University
000 University Avenue South
Ottawa, ON X1Y 2Z3

Dear P. J. Jones:

On November 28, 2005, I submitted a manuscript entitled "In Defence of the Doctoral Dissertation" to your office for publication. On January 7, 2006, I sent a follow-up letter requesting information on the status of my manuscript. As well, I enclosed a second title page, three (3) more copies of my manuscript, and another self-addressed, stamped envelope. To date, I have not received a response. Unfortunately, much of the material in the paper is time sensitive. Hence, I would appreciate a prompt reply. In short, has my work been reviewed, is it presently under review, or will it be reviewed shortly?

Yours truly,

G. Patrick O'Neill, Ph.D.

Figure 7-5. An example of a second follow-up letter.

Figure 7-6 is seen as a last resort. It should be used only when you decide that you have nothing to lose. Begin by reprimanding the editor. Let the person know that you are disappointed. You have been ignored and nobody likes to be ignored. Remind them of their obligations and close with an ultimatum. Either the editor acknowledges by a set date, or you will send your manuscript elsewhere. The time allotted will depend on the distance of the publisher from your workplace. Typically, you might allow 4 working days for transit (2 forward & 2 return) and 6 for the response, for a total of 10 working days.

January 25, 2006

P. J. Jones, Editor
Canadian Journal of Research
Canuck University
000 University Avenue South
Ottawa, ON X1Y 2Z3

Dear P. J. Jones:

Re: *In Defence of the Doctoral Dissertation*

As I begin to write this letter, I wonder what approach I should take. I am strongly tempted to grieve my case with your dean. *(At the same time, however, I do not wish to upset the editor as it might distract from her sense of objectivity.)*

I do believe, though, that a response on your part is warranted as you have had my paper since last December. I requested an update on the status of my manuscript on January 7, but you chose to ignore my letter. I realize that you are extremely busy and that reviews can take 5 or 6 months, but at this stage, I am not even sure that you will review my work.

I believe that you, as the editor of the *Journal*, have some obligation to your clients. That obligation, at least, should entail a courteous acknowledgement. I have decided, therefore, that either you acknowledge my correspondence within **ten** (10) working days from the date of this letter, or I will send my manuscript to another journal.

Yours truly,

G. Patrick O'Neill, Ph.D.

Figure 7-6. An example of a final follow-up letter.

Despite your best efforts, you may not get a response. Silence is usually an indication that either the journal has become insolvent or that you have made a poor choice.

If you receive an acknowledgement, it will be either a card or a form letter like that shown in Figure 7-7. Most editors will thank you for your manuscript, give some indication of the time required for the review process, and stipulate the preconditions under which your manuscript will be reviewed. As stressed in paragraph two, this publisher assumes (a) that the work is original, (b) that it has not or will not be published elsewhere, and (c) that it is not presently under review for publication elsewhere.

DATE:

ADDRESSEE:

SALUTATION:

RE: (in reference to)

Thank you for submitting your manuscript for possible publication in the *Canadian Journal of Research*. Your manuscript will be sent for blind review. Two independent reviewers will be selected on the basis of recommendations from our Editorial Board. On receipt of the reviewers' reports, we shall inform you of our decision and send you copies of their comments. The review process normally takes about 6 months.

In accepting your manuscript for review and possible publication in *CJR*, we assume that the work is original except where you acknowledge otherwise, that it is not or will not be published elsewhere, and that it is not now under consideration for publication elsewhere. If these assumptions are incorrect, please let me know immediately.

We appreciate your interest in *CJR*.

Yours sincerely,

P. J. Jones
Editor

Figure 7-7. A sample letter of acknowledgement.

Accepting the Verdict

The review period varies considerably from journal to journal. Some reviews take 3 to 6 months; others take longer. It is a slow process because most editors have other responsibilities. Most have to teach and many are actively involved in their own research projects. Thus, they may devote only 1 or 2 days a week to their editorial duties. As a result, "it may take some time before an initial screening is completed and reviewers are assigned" (Natriello, 1996, p. 511). One or more of the reviewers may even "decline and so new reviewers will have to be identified" (p. 511). In addition, reviewers are sometimes remiss; they have to be continually reminded, prodded, and, in extreme cases, coerced. "Some reviewers never return reviews" (p. 511).

The review is based on evaluation criteria which normally are not weighted or listed in order of importance. There is no prescribed number, but the following are typical:

1. Accuracy (correct)
2. Adequacy (complete)
3. Clarity (concrete)
4. Consistency (uniform)
5. Continuity (connected)
6. Objectivity (rational)
7. Originality (novel)
8. Significance (important)
9. Interest level (relevant)
10. Readership level (appropriate).

Some journals use checklists and comments, some use rating scales and comments, and some use comments only. Most ask for a balanced assessment. As well, reviewers are sometimes reminded of their professional responsibilities. An unpublished manuscript, for instance, is a privileged document. As such, it is unethical to cite from it or use it to advance your own work without the consent of the author(s) (see Chapter 9). A cover letter with a standard review form is given in Figure 7-8.

Dr. Warren O. Eaton, Editor   *(204) 474-9739*
Canadian Journal of Behavioural   *(204) 474-7599 [Fax]*
*   Science*   *Warren_Eaton@Umanitoba.CA*
Department of Psychology
University of Manitoba
Winnipeg, Manitoba R3T 2N2

[Date]

File No. [manuscript number]

[reviewer & address]

Dear Dr.   :

Thank you for agreeing to review the enclosed manuscript, which has been submitted to the *Canadian Journal of Behavioural Science* for possible publication. The *Journal* relies on the appraisals of consultants like you to reach an editorial decision, and I look forward to receiving your evaluation of this work.

CJBS publishes original contributions in areas of abnormal, behavioural, clinical, community, counseling, developmental, educational, organization-al, personality, and social psychology. Manuscripts recommended for acceptance should meet high levels of scientific standards. Empirical findings should be placed within a clear conceptual framework, designed well, analyzed appropriately, and interpreted soundly. In addition, the paper should be written so as to be accessible to the *Journal*'s diverse readership.

Remember that this manuscript is a privileged communication. Neither cite it prior to its publication, nor use the information it contains for unfair advancement of your own research.

Thank you for your cooperation.

Yours sincerely,

Warren Eaton, Ph.D.

A Journal of the Canadian Psychological Association / Une revue de la Société canadienne de psychologie

Canadian Journal of Behavioural Science
Confidential Memorandum from Reviewer to Editor
Warren Eaton, Department of Psychology, Univ. of Manitoba, Winnipeg, MB R3T 2N2
E-mail: Warren_Eaton@umanitoba.ca   Fax: (204) 474-7599

Please prepare written comments that can be shared with the author(s) and other reviewers and append them to this page. *This* page will be seen only by the editor.

Reviewer A:

Date Sent:

File #:

Title:

Summary appraisal of ms	Excellent	Good	Adequate	Poor	NA
Adequacy of literature review	____	____	____	____	____
Adequacy of design & analysis	____	____	____	____	____
Interpretation of results	____	____	____	____	____
Clarity of communication	____	____	____	____	____
Likelihood of future citation	____	____	____	____	____
Appropriateness for CJBS	____	____	____	____	____

Overall recommendation

____   Accept outright.

____   Accept with revisions as indicated (additional review not required).

____   Reject, but recommend resubmission following revision or inclusion of more data (revised ms. to be reviewed again before a final decision is made).

____   Reject. Please provide basis for rejection in your report. If another outlet would be more appropriate, please identify the journal here: .

Please return your review by

Remarks (confidential to Editor).

Figure 7-8. A cover letter with a standard review form. (Reprinted with permission of the Canadian Psychological Association.)

The verdict is usually summarized in one of four possible recommendations: accept as is, accept with minor revisions, accept subject to major revisions, or reject. Rarely is a paper accepted as is; most require minor or major revisions. Minor revisions are good news; your paper is publishable; it needs some repair, but generally it is of good quality. At first, some of the remarks may seem trivial. If so, set them aside for a few days; then reread them. As a rule, you will find that most do improve the quality of your work.

You do not have to incorporate all the reviewers' suggestions, but should include obvious errors, those on which the editor insists, and those on which there is unanimity. Others are open to debate, especially if contradictory. Always provide a rationale for your stance. Be sure that your arguments are presented in a professional manner. There is no need for angry outbursts or personal attacks on the editor or the reviewers.

Captions to be included in your cover letter are given in Figure 7-9. State your purpose and format in the introduction, list your revisions and your objections in the body, and close on a positive note.

Divide the body into two parts. First, list your revisions, and second, list your objections. Proceed from the beginning of the paper to the end; do not jump around. Address all comments; do not be selective. Note the reviewer's suggestion, give its exact location, and state your revision or objection.

Major revisions are bad news; your paper may be publishable, but it needs an overhaul; generally it is of poor quality. You will have to decide: Are the revisions worth the effort? You could go to the trouble of making the changes and still get rejected, particularly if the revisions are sent back to the reviewers who can, and often do, make additional demands on the author. This cycle can continue for several months and, in some cases, a year or more.

ৰ৶ৰ৶ৡ৶ৡ৶

Your manuscript is both good and original; but the part that is good is not original, and the part that is original is not good.

Samuel Johnson

ৰ৶ৰ৶ৡ৶ৡ৶

LETTERHEAD

DATE:

ADDRESSEE:

SALUTATION:

RE: (in reference to)

INTRODUCTION: Enclosed are the corrections for my article entitled "In Defence of the Doctoral Dissertation." The letter is divided into two parts. The first part lists those areas in which changes were made. The second part lists those areas in which changes were not made.

BODY:

I *Number and List Revisions* (additions, corrections, deletions)

    1. (a) Referee's suggestion, page 2
        (b) Your revision

    2. (a) Referee's suggestion, page 10
        (b) Your revision

    3. And so on.

II *Number and List Objections*

    1. (a) Referee's suggestion, page 3
        (b) Your objection

    2. (a) Referee's suggestion, page 7
        (b) Your objection

    3. And so on.

CLOSING: I trust that this version will meet with your approval.

Figure 7-9. Captions to be included in a cover letter accompanying revisions.

Rejection slips are blunt and to the point. They do not say perhaps, possibly, or maybe. They say "No!" Initially, you may be shattered, but it is best to accept the verdict as it is rarely reversed. The slip is usually in the form of a letter outlining the reasons for the rejection. The letters often contain insensitive comments and blatant crudities such as the editor's signature initialled by an unknown assistant. Choice phrases include: "I regret that I have to inform you that...," "I am sorry to inform you that...," "I am afraid that...," or "Unfortunately, our referees do not recommend that...." In short, it is "thanks but no thanks." Regardless, you should not be discouraged. Everyone gets rejected (Day, 1996; Henson, 1999; Thyer, 1994).

> To attempt to publish articles in scholarly journals is by definition to subject yourself to the experience of receiving letters of rejection. Both novice and experienced academics and practitioners find their works to be rejected on a regular basis, which is not a surprise because some journals have a greater than 90% rejection rate. This is not a cause for shame or regret. (Thyer, 1994, p. 55)

Besides, you can profit from the experience. Study the feedback, make notes, and "welcome the opportunity to revise as a learning experience; it's a positive activity, not one to fear or be embarrassed about" (Day, 1996, p. 16).

Repackage your manuscript and send it to your second-choice journal. You may wish to repeat this procedure until your piece is eventually accepted, but that depends on your sense of self. Normally, you would abandon it after the third rejection. In fact, it is strongly recommended that you do so. Perhaps parts could be salvaged and used in another paper. Still, there are those who maintain that any publication is better than no publication; that, in essence, everything counts. If your department subscribes to this view, then as a last resort, you might revise it and send it to a newsletter.

An acceptance slip does not mean that the ordeal is over. A paper can remain *in press* for another 3 to 6 months depending on the backlog of accepted papers. Most journals publish only three or four issues a year. Hence, the time from first submission to final publication can be anywhere from 1 to 2 years.

Checking Proofs

As a last step, you may be asked to proofread the printer's proof (i.e., the typeset copy of your manuscript). Proofs come in one of two forms, galley proofs (galleys) or page proofs. Both are set as they will appear in print; the former in long, single columns; the latter in pages.

You will receive the printer's proof about 6 to 8 weeks before the publication deadline. On average, you will have a week from the date of receipt to check the copy (see Figure 7-10). You should arrange to have a "dependable" colleague check your proofs if you are away. If you fail to return them on time, one of two things could happen. The editor could either publish the piece without the corrections or pull the piece from the lineup. The first scenario could be a big embarrassment, the second a big disappointment.

DATE:

ADDRESSEE:

SALUTATION:

RE: (in reference to)

Enclosed are the galleys of your article which is scheduled to be published in "x" issue of *CJR*.

Please proofread them carefully and return them by courier to the above address within **one** week of receipt. All corrections should be made on the copy. Restrict your corrections to typesetting errors. Please use a *red* pen.

Twenty-five reprints will be provided free of charge. Additional copies may be requested by submitting the Reprint Order Form below along with appropriate payment.

Sincerely,

P. J. Jones
Editor

Reprint Order Form

Reprints must be ordered in minimum lots of 100. Costs are calculated on the length of your article and on the number ordered. All prices are quoted in Canadian (Cdn.) dollars. Please refer to the enclosed chart for details.

Author:

Title of article:

Volume: Issue: Date:

I wish to order _____ additional reprints at a cost of _____ .

For delivery outside Canada:

    1. Add 10% for regular mail ☐
    2. Add 15% for air mail   ☐

Enclosed is a cheque or money order in the amount of $_____ , payable to The Canadian Research Association.

Figure 7-10. A sample letter on proofreading instructions and on the ordering of reprints.

       Undertake two readings. The first reading should enlist the help of a colleague or friend. The person should read the original manuscript aloud while you check the proof. The reader should carefully enunciate each word and numeral, stress each punctuation sign, and accent the beginning and ending of each paragraph. As well, the reader should identify all headings and subheadings by level (i.e., Level 2, Level 3, etc.), indicate where illustrations go (e.g., Insert Table 1 about here), and detail the contents of all figures and tables. Check for typographical errors—incorrect capitalization, incorrect or missing punctuation, missing words, misspelled words, and redundant words.
       You are encouraged to use conventional proofreader's marks (see Figure 7-11). If you are unfamiliar with the symbols, strike the word or mark the spot with a caret (^) in the column of type and draw an arrow out to the margin. Here, make your correction. Never make interlinear changes (i.e., above or below the line of type) as, inevitably, some will be missed.

Instruction	Margin Mark	Instruction	Margin Mark
Align horizontally	⹀	Insert quotation marks	⹂/⹂
Align vertically	‖	Insert semicolon	⌃;
Broken letter	✕	Insert space	#
Capitalize letter	(cap)	Insert word	# for #
Centre	⊐⊏	Let it stand	(stet)
Close up space	⌒	Line break	⌐
Delete	ℓ	Move down	⊔
Delete and close up	℮	Move left	⊏
Flush left	(fl)	Move right	⊐
Flush right	(fr)	Move up	⊓
Indent	▭	Run paragraphs together	(no ¶)
Insert apostrophe	⌄	Set in boldface type	(bf)
Insert asterisk	⋆	Set in italic type	(ital)
Insert brackets	[/]	Set in lightface type	(lf)
Insert colon	(⦂)	Set in lowercase	(lc)
Insert comma	⌃	Set in roman type	(rom)
Insert dagger	†	Spell out	(sp)
Insert double dagger	‡	Start new paragraph	¶
Insert em dash	$\frac{1}{M}$	Subscript	⋀

Insert en dash	$\frac{1}{N}$	Superscript	V
Insert hyphen	|=|	Transpose	(tr)
Insert parentheses	(/)	Turn right side up	⊙
Insert period	⊙	Virgule (solidus)	/
Insert question mark	?	Wrong font	(wf)

Note. The proofreader's marks used in Canada were established by the American National Standards Institute. Figure 7-11 is not an exhaustive list, but it does contain the most common marks or symbols. Some of the marks may differ from those used in other countries, but generally they are understood worldwide.

Figure 7-11. Conventional proofreader's marks.

If a line is missing, type it on a slip of paper and tape it to the proof. Flag it and draw an arrow to show where it goes. Do not, however, make any unnecessary changes. If you insist, you could be charged. The proofs are sent to be corrected, not rewritten.

The colour of your marks should be different from those of the typeset text. A red pen, particularly a fine point, is recommended. Do not use a felt tip marker. Anything not to be typeset, such as special notes to the editor, should be circled. This helps editors distinguish between instructions to them and changes required to the text.

Do the second reading yourself. Go slowly. Focus on each word rather than on the meaning of the text. Cross-check all numbers and symbols in the text against those in the tables. Cross-check the references in the text against those in the reference list. Check your illustrations for broken lines, faulty alignment, and correct data. Check the title and the running head for accuracy and consistency. Check the spelling of your name, your institution, and its address. Transcription errors sometimes occur here. For example, St. Catharines, Ontario is often spelled St. Catherines, that is, with an "e" rather than an "a".

Return your proofs by courier. Enclose a cover letter which

1. States the purpose of your correspondence,
2. Answers "all" questions raised by the editor,
3. Explains major errors and their corrections,
4. Thanks the editor.

Ordering Reprints

You should receive two or more complimentary copies of the issue in which your article appears. Or as indicated in Figure 7-10, you may receive free reprints with the added option of ordering additional sets at so much a set. The reprint order form is usually sent with the proofs. If the form was not included, e-mail or telephone the publisher as the omission was probably an oversight.

How many reprints should you order? If uncertain, order extra copies because they may be unavailable later, and they will cost more. You usually order in lots of 50 or 100. The publisher will include a reprint price list chart. Prices are listed on a grid. The grid is based on a dual sliding scale. On the one hand, the price increases with the number of printed pages per article. On the other hand, the price per unit decreases with the size of the order. That is, a lot of 300 would cost less per reprint than a lot of 100. After lots of 300 or more, the cost per unit is fixed at a lower rate. In other words, you can buy an additional 100 copies, beyond the first 300, at a fraction of the price that you would pay for the first 100.

After your article is published, you may receive requests for free reprints. It is exciting to know that your work is being read across the country, in Africa, in Asia, in Europe, and around the world. Figure 7-12 is a typical reprint request card. The card should specify the article requested, identify the sender, and include a return, self-addressed, adhesive label.

હ્ય~હ્ય~ઉ~ઉ

Patience is bitter, but its fruit is sweet.

Jean-Jacques Rousseau

હ્ય~હ્ય~ઉ~ઉ

Dear _____

Please send _____ reprint(s) of your recent article entitled,

_____

_____

Which appeared in _____

Vol. _____, No. _____, Pages _____, Year _____.

Any related material would also be appreciated. A mailing label is provided for your convenience.

Thank you.

Wei Sun
No. 3 Building
Hong Lian Bei Cun
Haidian District
Beijing, CHINA
100088

Mailing Label

Figure 7-12. A typical reprint request card.

Chapter Eight

Books and Book Reviews

Of all the needs a book has, the chief need is that it be readable.

Anthony Trollope

Types of Books

*T*here are three types of books: scholarly books, textbooks, and trade (popular) books. The distinction between the first two is sometimes blurred as "scholarly monographs and collections of articles are sometimes used as supplementary or even main texts in a college course" (Luey, 2002, p. 126). Regardless, the primary purpose of scholarly books is to advance knowledge. The knowledge can be research-based, theory-based, or both. In contrast, textbooks

> rarely represent the culmination of research or what is traditionally considered "scholarly" activity. Instead, they summarize, organize, and analyze the accumulated wisdom of an area of knowledge, presenting it in a way that is comprehensible to students at a specific level of competence. (p. 126)

Trade books are "mass-market audience books" (Cantor, 1993, p. 119). They include hardback (hardbound, hardcover) and paperback (softbound, softcover) editions on almost every imaginable topic: art, business, computers, health, history, music, religion, science, sports, travel, and so on. They are sold in airports, bookstores, department stores, drugstores, and supermarkets. Some make the best-seller list.

The text of a scholarly book can be authored, compiled, edited, or translated. An authored book is an original volume written by one or more persons. A compiled book, often called an anthology, contains reprinted material. The work is commissioned by a compiler who selects items based on personal needs or the needs of a publisher. The contributors to special collections are usually renowned individuals, but need not be. Their selection hinges on many factors of which prestige, power, and popularity are three.

An edited book, often called a contributor text or a book of readings, contains a central theme on which either individual articles or chapters are written. Those written in honour of a particular scholar are called festschrifts.

A translated book is a volume that has been translated from one language into another. Some of the Great Books of the Western World, for example, have been translated from Latin into English.

Most textbooks and trade books are authored, but some are compiled, edited, or translated. They are used for either required or supplementary reading. College and university textbooks can be either introductory or advanced. Introductory books are general, advanced books are subject-specific.

Types of Publishers

There are six types of presses: university, societal, commercial scholarly, textbook, trade, and vanity. University and societal presses are not-for-profit (nonprofit) publishers. The rest are for-profit publishers. University presses vary in size. Some publish 5 books a year, others publish 25 books a year. Some publish in special fields, others publish across fields. Some publish on national issues, others publish on regional issues. Some do both. Some cater to academics only, others cater to both academics and the public-at-large.

Their primary purpose is to disseminate scholarly knowledge. Most will absorb losses. They can afford losses because their presses are subsidized. Most rely on internal funding as well as grants from public agencies and private foundations.

High standards are the norm. Manuscripts are subjected to rigorous peer review, both inside and outside the host institution. Once accepted, a manuscript must go through a series of carefully monitored steps to ensure quality control in design and production.

Societal presses are sponsored by professional associations that cater to particular groups. Their quality varies greatly as do their review processes. Some are peer-reviewed, others are not. Most are reputable, many are prestigious. Their marketing resources are limited, but they sometimes compensate by arranging for distribution through larger university presses. They range in size from local affiliates to national and international organizations.

Commercial scholarly presses are in direct competition with university presses. Both disseminate new scholarship, but the former publish for profit. This means that they are more selective in what they publish. They often target specific divisions within the university. For instance, some might focus on the life sciences, others might focus on the physical sciences, and still others might focus on the social sciences.

In general, commercial scholarly presses have two advantages over university presses. First, their production time is shorter, but their quality varies more than that of university presses.

> Some expend a great deal of effort on editing, while some do only the most cursory correction of punctuation. Some routinely win industry prizes for design and production, while others add minimal design to disks supplied by the author. (Luey, 2002, p. 52)

Second, their marketing and sales team is more aggressive. They exhibit their books at conferences, they advertise in professional magazines and scientific journals, and they target individuals. In addition, they often maintain their presence in international markets through subsidiary companies and agreements with foreign distributors.

Textbook publishers are commercial firms that produce elementary, high school, college, and university textbooks. They may also produce instructor's manuals, software materials, study guides, test banks, and so forth. Some have divisions. For example, some might have a college division or a humanities division.

Textbook publishing is big business. Companies continually monitor national and international markets for shifts and trends in instructional materials. Their goal is to turn a profit. Thus, the industry generally "has an aura far removed from that of academe" (p. 129).

> Acquiring editors tend to be different sorts of people than university press editors. Usually they have arrived in the acquisitions department via sales and marketing rather than manuscript editing or academia. If all publishers are on a continuum between the worlds of scholarship and business, textbook editors are closer to the business end. (p. 128)

Trade houses are commercial presses whose readership is the general public. Their market "is high risk and ever changing" (Cantor, 1993, p. 120). Profit is their guiding principle. Most will not invest in a book that has limited sales potential.

Vanity presses, sometimes called subsidy presses, publish for a fee. Most will publish on any topic if you are willing to pay for the design, the production, and the marketing. Often, they mimic genuine publishers, but they are impostors. Publication is based strictly on your pocketbook. You absorb all the costs and assume all the risks. "No editorial or expert judgment enters the picture. For this reason, publication by a vanity press carries *no* prestige and *no* [italics added] clout with tenure committees" (Luey, 2002, p. 55) in legitimate (i.e., accredited) universities.

Developing a Prospectus

A prospectus is a preliminary proposal for a book. You need one whether you intend to write, compile, or edit a book. Some publishers provide guidelines, others do not. A typical prospectus can be divided into three areas: the description of the book, the description of the market, and the description of the author(s).

The description of the book should be divided into four parts:

1. Discuss your book.

    ❖ What kind of book is it?
    ❖ What is the major theme?
    ❖ What is the approach?
    ❖ What are the main features?
    ❖ What is the approximate length?
    ❖ Will there be illustrations? If so, how many?

2. Provide a rationale.

   ❖ Why this book?
   ❖ Is there a need for the book?
   ❖ What purpose will it serve?

3. Provide an outline.

   ❖ Furnish a table of contents.
   ❖ Include two chapters; preferably the second chapter and an end chapter.
   ❖ Sketch the remaining chapters.

4. Include a time line.

   ❖ Note how much is written.
   ❖ Indicate a completion date.

The description of the market should be divided into two parts:

1. Identify the consumer.

   ❖ Who will buy the book?
   ❖ To whom is it directed?
   ❖ What is the grade level?
   ❖ What courses, in particular, might use it?
   ❖ How often are the courses offered?
   ❖ What is the average enrolment?

Your information must "be as specific as possible in describing the target audience. Books that purport to be used in three or four or even five different courses frequently end up being adopted in none" (Smith, 1997, p. 98).

2. Compare the competition.

   ❖ Is your book better?
   ❖ Is your book bigger?

Give details. Be assertive. You are the expert. You must convince the publisher that you know the demands of the market, and that your book will meet them.

> A good textbook proposal will show exactly what niche the author
> is aiming for, what that segment's needs are that the text's features
> will address directly, and what the strengths and weaknesses of the
> existing competition are. (p. 100)

The description of the author(s) should be divided into four parts:

1. Report research conducted in the area.
2. List recent publications in the area.
3. List courses taught in the area.

   ❖ Include syllabuses,
   ❖ Include course numbers,
   ❖ Include dates,
   ❖ Include enrolment figures.

4. Document reaction to material used in class.

   ❖ Include course evaluations,
   ❖ Include testimonials,
   ❖ Include informal correspondence (e.g., notes, thank
     you cards, unsolicited letters, etc.).

The publisher may ask to see your curriculum vitae. The objective is to
establish your credibility. Are you qualified to write, compile, or edit
the book?

Selecting a Publisher

You must pick publishers that publish in your field; otherwise, you will
be wasting your time. You will need a literary agent if your book is a
trade book. Reputable agents can be found in the latest annual edition
of the *Guide to Literary Agents* (see Publisher Directories in Appendix
H). The *Guide* gives you their addresses, their telephone numbers, the
type of work handled and preferred, recent sales, their reading fees (if
any), and their commission on sales. They will assess the potential of
your manuscript, they will submit your work to publishers, and they will

negotiate contracts, but they will not revise or edit your manuscript; that is your responsibility. They may, however, recommend a ghostwriter, a copy editor, or a proofreader. Each will charge a separate fee.

Finding a publisher for a scholarly book or textbook requires three steps. First, check the most recent volume of *Books in Print* to see who has published in your field (see Publisher Directories in Appendix H). Second, check the current *Writer's Market* for a description of each company (see Publisher Directories in Appendix H). The description includes information on the number of titles published per year, the percentage of first-time authors, royalty rates, and so on. Third, go to the stacks and examine recent editions. Check the binding, the cover, the design, the layout, the printing, the graphics, and the index. Are their books well-made? Are they attractive? Are they easy to read? Would you use them?

෯෯෯෯

Books, like men, are subject to manners, behaviour; they are well or ill bred; well dressed or badly dressed.

Holbrook Jackson

෯෯෯෯

Select 10 prospective publishers. Base your selection on age, quality, and size. If the quality is equal, consider age and size. Bigger is not necessarily better although it does have some advantages. Larger presses, for instance, have more in-house specialists who can offer technical support in design, editing, and graphics. As well, they have the resources to promote and market a book more widely. Of course, big also has disadvantages. For example, you may be faced with more layers of bureaucracy. Decision-making may be more formal, more complex, and more intense. Your work could get lost, misplaced, or relegated to the bottom of a pile.

In contrast, smaller houses may have only one or two editors. Decisions are made more quickly and production time is faster, but the quality will vary more because they contract out much of their work.

Despite their differences, larger presses, as a rule, carry more prestige than smaller presses. And old, established presses, whether large or small, carry more prestige than newer presses. Ideally, then, you should select large, established presses, but there are other factors to consider. Ask yourself: Why are you writing the book? Is it to

1. Advance your career?
2. Become an authority?
3. Enhance your reputation?
4. Fulfill a dream?
5. Make money?

Select old, established presses if numbers 2 and 3 are paramount. Select large, international presses if number 5 is paramount. Select small, commercial presses if you are in a hurry to advance your career or fulfill a dream.

Rank order your 10 selections. The top five become your first-choice presses. Prepare a query letter. The letter should be carefully crafted, as it is a reflection of your writing abilities. Send the letter to the editor-in-chief (sometimes called the editorial director) or to the acquisitions editor, or to the division editor of each press.

Divide the letter into four paragraphs. Introduce yourself in the first paragraph, state your purpose, and note why you selected their press. Briefly explain the project in the second paragraph (refer to the enclosed prospectus). Describe the book's saleability in the third paragraph (refer to the enclosed prospectus). The last paragraph should be candid. If you have contacted other publishers, say so. You can send a query letter to more than one press at the same time, but it is unethical to have two presses review a complete manuscript at the same time, unless both are aware of it and agree to it. End by thanking the editor.

Send each package by courier. Use a padded envelope, seal the ends, record the date, and keep a disk copy and a hard copy of everything in a safe place.

You should receive an acknowledgement within 2 to 4 weeks. Reviews take about 3 to 6 months. Some may not reply. E-mail or call those that do not respond. If they ignore you, send a follow-up letter. Be polite, but firm. Give them an ultimatum. Set a response date. If they ignore it, withdraw your submission. Ask them to return your prospectus and the two chapters, and to destroy all copies.

You may not get an offer on the first round. This is to be

expected, especially if you are a first-time author. Try again. Three or four rounds are not uncommon. Norman and Streiner (1997), for example, "approached approximately 25 publishers" (p. xi) before they were successful.

Negotiating a Contract

A contract is a legal document that spells out the roles, rights, and responsibilities of the author and the publisher. It signals the beginning of a long-term relationship between two parties. The publisher provides a range of services in exchange for rights to your work. The rights can be limited or exclusive. Limited rights are basic rights. Exclusive rights include basic rights and subsidiary rights. Basic rights include the right to publish your work in book form in the English language and distribute it in Canada, in North America, or throughout the English-speaking world. Subsidiary rights are the rights to license rights to others. There are four types of licences. First, the publisher may license foreign language rights (translations into Chinese, German, Spanish, etc.). Second, the publisher may license reprint rights (abridgements, anthologies, book clubs, etc.). Third, the publisher may license first and second serial rights (compendiums and extracts in journals, magazines, newspapers, etc.). First serial rights are licences negotiated before publication; second serial rights are licences negotiated after publication. Fourth, the publisher may license electronic rights (CD-ROMs, radio, television, etc.).

The standard contract usually has side headings. It begins with definitions, thereafter the headings vary. Typical headings include Delivery, Copyright, Warranties, Acceptability, Auxiliary Material, Proofs, Permissions, Design, Author's Copies, Subsidiary Rights, Royalties, Accounting, Advertising and Marketing, Out of Print, Revised Editions, Option for New Work, and so forth. Some items are negotiable, others are not. "You should read every word, and you shouldn't assume fairness" (Henson, 1999, p. 218). If you are confused, seek counsel from a lawyer who specializes in intellectual property law. Check the latest annual edition of *The Book Trade in Canada* for a list of Canadian law firms that deal with copyright, libel, and media law (see Publisher Directories in Appendix H). They can review, interpret, and possibly amend sections of the contract to your advantage. Be sure that you understand each clause and its implications before you sign the contract.

What is negotiable? Copyright is not normally negotiable, but it depends on the book. Sometimes publishers are not interested in subsidiary rights. They are only interested in the right to publish your book in a hardback (hb) or paperback (pb) edition. This, though, is rare. As a rule, you will not secure a contract unless you assign (sell) all your rights to the publisher. As a safeguard, however, you can negotiate a termination clause. The clause allows you to reclaim the basic publication rights and all other rights not yet sold or licensed if the publisher lets the book go out of stock and refuses to reprint it within a specified time. You may also wish to have some of the subsidiary rights revert back to you after 5 years if the publisher fails to market the work in other countries or in other forms.

You can negotiate the number of free copies and your discount price on additional copies. Most publishers will offer you 5 free copies; you might ask for 10. Additional copies should be sold to you at a discount. Discounts range from 25 to 50 percent off the publisher's retail list price. You might ask for 50 percent. The books are for the author's use only; they are not for resale.

In addition, you might negotiate the right to purchase other books published by the publisher at a 30 percent discount from the retail price, plus shipping and handling. Again, the books are for the author's use only; they are not for resale.

You can negotiate the length of the manuscript, within reason, and the delivery date of the completed work. You can also negotiate the period between acceptance of the manuscript and publication of the manuscript. Some publishers ignore this clause or retain complete control by stating only that they will publish the work within a reasonable time. But, what is reasonable? Eight to 12 months is reasonable. "Get it in writing."

You can negotiate the right-of-first-refusal on your next work. Right-of-first-refusal means that you "must" share your next book with this publisher first. If they decline it, then, and only then, are you at liberty to approach other publishers. This precondition, however, may restrict your ability to properly exploit your wares, especially if your next work is unrelated to the present volume. You might ask the publisher to drop this clause.

You can negotiate revised editions. The publisher can request revisions to the work at any time. If, for some reason, you are unable or unwilling to make the revisions, the publisher may have the right to commission the work, to charge the costs against your royalties, and to cease using your name after the first set of revisions. This means, in essence, that unless you protect yourself, you could in time lose complete control over the work. Insist that two safety clauses be inserted, one that protects your name and one that protects your work. The first clause should ensure that your name is always on the work; that you will always be credited as the first author of the work. The second clause should stipulate that no changes can be made to the work without the expressed consent of both the author and the publisher.

You can negotiate royalties. Royalties on scholarly books and textbooks are usually calculated as a percentage of net sales. Net is the cash amount received by the publisher from each copy of the work sold and not returned after discounts and expenses. The range for scholarly books is 6 to 10 percent; the range for textbooks is 10 to 18 percent. Royalties on trade books are paid on the retail price. The range is 5 to 10 percent. Royalties on foreign sales are about one-half, on average, of domestic sales because of the higher shipping and handling costs.

Sometimes a publisher will offer a flat fee for the rights to a compiled or edited volume. Generally, this is an accepted practice, but it is not recommended for authored volumes, with one exception. A nonprofit press, such as a societal press, for instance, may offer a fixed fee because of budget constraints. In this case, you might consider the offer as it is understood: What you lose in royalties you gain in prestige.

Royalties may be based on either a fixed scale or an escalating scale. A fixed scale means that you get the same percentage regardless of the number of units sold. An escalating scale, on the other hand, increases your percentage in proportion to the number of units sold. You might, for example, get 5 percent on the first two thousand copies, 8 percent on the next four thousand copies, and 15 percent thereafter. Some companies pay no royalties on the first one thousand copies while others place time restrictions on the number sold. For instance, the scale could be contingent on the sale of a certain number of units within a period, often a year. In other words, total sales are counted on an annual basis; they are not cumulative over the lifetime of the contract. The dollar difference can be large. For example, suppose that the publisher sold eight thousand copies in the first year. This means that you would get 5 percent on the first two thousand copies, 8 percent on the next four thousand copies, and 15 percent on the remaining two thousand copies. Suppose that the publisher sells two thousand additional copies in the second year. Your total sales for the 2 years are now ten thousand copies. If your sales were cumulative, you would get 15 percent on the additional two thousand copies. If they were annual, you would only get 5 percent on the additional two thousand copies. What is the dollar difference? On a net receipt of $50.00 a unit, the difference is a "whopping" $10,000. If your royalty is 15 percent, the return would be $7.50 a unit. If your royalty is 5 percent, the return would be $2.50 a unit. This is a difference of $5.00 a unit. Thus, on a sale of two thousand units, the difference is $15,000 - $5,000 = $10,000.

If you have a choice between a fixed scale or an escalating scale, choose the fixed scale. According to Henson (1999),

> a sliding scale can be advantageous to the author when the book's market is large and the book sells well. But publishing companies assess the potential sales of a given book and design variable scales that favor themselves. I therefore believe that beginning writers are far better off with a fixed rate. (p. 219)

Authors receive about one half (50%) of all royalties from subsidiary revenues. This can vary greatly, though, depending on how the work is exploited.

Fulfilling Your Obligations

The contract will outline your responsibilities as they relate to preparation of the manuscript (delivery date, length, number of copies), permissions, editing, proofing, indexing, and marketing. These duties can be divided into three stages: the preproduction stage, the production stage, and the postproduction stage. Your primary preproduction task is to write and deliver a complete manuscript, acceptable to the publisher, by a specific date. The publisher will use an in-house style manual or recommend one (see Appendix B). You must follow it exactly. The manual will provide information on abbreviations, footnotes, headings, illustrations, numbering, punctuation, references, spacing, spelling, and so forth. As well, the publisher may supply you with writing tips similar to those discussed in Chapters 2, 4, and 5. Be sure to read them. They may also instruct you on how to set up the front matter and the back matter. A complete manuscript would include most, but not necessarily all, of the following parts:

Front Matter

1. A half title page (supplied by publisher)
2. A title page
3. A copyright page (supplied by publisher)
4. A dedication (if one)
5. A list of contributors (compiled and edited volumes only)
6. A table of contents
7. A list of figures (if any)
8. A list of tables (if any)
9. A foreword (if one)
10. A preface (if one)
11. Acknowledgements (if any)

Text

1. The chapters
2. Epilogue (if one)

Back Matter

1. Notes (if any)
2. Appendix or appendices (if any)
3. Glossary (if one)
4. Bibliography or references
5. Index (to be submitted later).

Permissions are your responsibility. The publisher should provide guidelines on when to request them, and on how to obtain them. They may supply you with a request form and a permissions log. You will be asked to submit the signed letters of request, the permissions log, and the copies requested along with your manuscript. Chapter 9 discusses this topic in more detail. If you are unclear, ask the acquisitions editor for help.

Normally, the author is expected to pay all permission fees. You might ask the publisher to share the cost. If they refuse, ask them to advance the fees out of your royalty account. Some contracts state that the publisher is authorized to acquire permissions that the author does not obtain. The word *authorized* is dangerous, especially if the costs are excessive. Ask that a ceiling be placed on the costs that are charged to you and that all additional, auxiliary material commissioned by the publisher be paid for by the publisher, not by you.

Your manuscript will be reviewed by a team of experts. They will check for accuracy, clarity, consistency, continuity, objectivity, originality, and so on. The publisher will review their comments and ask you to revise certain sections by a specific date. Once your revisions are completed, and approved by the acquisitions editor, your manuscript will move to the production stage.

You have three responsibilities in the production stage.

1. You must check the copy-edited manuscript,
2. You must proofread the printer's proof, and
3. You must prepare an index or have someone prepare one for you.

The production editor will assign your manuscript to a copy editor who will go over it word by word, line by line, section by section. They will check for accuracy in grammar, spelling, and word usage. They will check for consistency in documentation, headings, punctuation, spacing, and the like. They will question assertions, tidy up figures and tables, remove unnecessary verbiage, insert transitions, shorten sentences, rearrange paragraphs, and in general, keep your text flowing smoothly.

ઈ•ઈ•ઈ•ઈ

A sentence should contain no unnecessary words, a paragraph no unnecessary sentences, for the same reason that a drawing should have no unnecessary lines and a machine no unnecessary parts.

William Strunk, Jr. and E. B. White

ઈ•ઈ•ઈ•ઈ

It is important that you check the copy-edited manuscript carefully because this is your last chance to make substantive changes without incurring charges. As a rule, corrections on the proofs are restricted to the typesetter's errors. You may, however, depending on your contract, be allowed additional changes provided they do not exceed 10 percent of the total cost of typesetting. If you exceed this figure, the cost will be deducted from your royalty account.

Work through the manuscript slowly; assess each deletion, weigh each addition, address each question. Has the message been distorted or lost? If you are uneasy about something or disagree with the copy editor, say so, but be diplomatic. It is better to be frank now than disappointed later. Let the production editor mediate disputes. Return the final copy-edited manuscript in person or by courier and keep a copy for your files. When the manuscript has been reworked to the satisfaction of the production editor, it will be sent to the typesetter.

At this stage, deadlines become crucial. Everything is interconnected. You must meet the typesetter's deadline, the typesetter must meet the printer's deadline, and the printer must meet the binder's deadline. Delays on your part can stall production for weeks or even months. Typesetting takes, on average, 4 to 8 weeks. You will receive a typeset copy of the manuscript called the printer's proof. The printer's proof comes in one of two forms, galley proofs (galleys) or page proofs. Both are set as they will appear in print; the former in long, single columns; the latter in pages. Some publishers use galleys and page proofs, others use only page proofs. A set of galleys will have headings and subheadings in place, but footnotes and illustrations may be grouped at the end of each chapter. You will receive specific instructions on how to proof the galleys and a return date. Two weeks is the norm. Remember, you must confine your corrections to typesetting errors; otherwise, you could be charged for costs incurred in changing the text.

Enlist some help. Have a friend read the copy-edited manuscript aloud while you check the galleys. You will be encouraged to use proofreader's marks (see Chapter 7). The reader should carefully enunciate each word and numeral, stress each punctuation sign, and accent the beginning and ending of each paragraph. As well, the reader should identify all headings and subheadings by level (i.e., Level 1, Level 2, etc.), cross-check all numbers and symbols in the text against those in the tables, cross-check the references in the text against those in the reference list, and check the tables for broken lines, faulty alignment, and missing data. In addition, the reader should check for typographical errors—incorrect capitalization, incorrect or missing punctuation, missing words, misspelled words, and redundant words.

To delete a word, draw a line through it and put the delete symbol in the left margin. To replace a word, draw a line through it and print the new word in the left margin. To add a word, draw a caret (^) in the line and print the new word in the left margin. To add a line, type it on a slip of paper and tape it to the proof. Flag it and draw an arrow to show where it goes.

Never make interlinear changes (i.e., above or below the line of type) as, inevitably, some will be missed. The colour of your marks should be different from those of the typeset text. A red pen, especially a fine point, is recommended. Do not use a felt tip marker. Anything not to be typeset, such as notes to the editor, should be circled. This helps editors distinguish between instructions to them and changes required to the text. Make a copy of all your corrections and return the galleys to the publisher on time.

Batches of page proofs will start arriving 3 to 4 weeks after you return the galleys. They will show everything in place, exactly as it will appear in the printed book. Proof each set as they arrive. Read the page proofs against the galleys. Always check the lines above and below each correction for new errors.

The author is responsible for preparing the index. You can either do it yourself or hire a professional indexer. If you are interested, the publisher may recommend one and let you know the cost. You and the production editor might meet with the indexer to discuss the type of index you want (author, subject, title, or a combination), its depth, and its breadth. The index is usually due in the publisher's office 2 to 3 weeks after you receive your last batch of page proofs.

If you decide to create the index yourself, read Chapter 18 entitled Indexes in *The Chicago Manual of Style* (see Appendix B) or check the Indexing Guides in Appendix H. There are several software programs available that will help you sort, cross-reference, and format your entries (e.g., Cindex, Macrex, & Sky Index). If you use one, check with your editor to ensure compatibility between your program and that of the typesetter's.

Your postproduction obligations are mainly promotional. You may be asked to write an abstract that will be placed in the publisher's catalogue and advertising material. You may also be asked to spend time at their book exhibits signing copies and promoting sales.

Book Reviews

Book reviews are short literary reports that condense and evaluate the contents of a book. Their quality varies greatly because they are not refereed (i.e., blindly reviewed). Thus, they are seen as "a relatively quick and painless way to [get] published" (Luey, 2002, p. 30), but, at the same time, they are not highly valued by promotion and tenure committees.

There are two types of reviews: solicited (invited) and un-solicited (uninvited). Solicited reviews are those in which the editor approaches you. Unsolicited are those in which you approach the editor. As a novice, you will have to take the latter approach; send a query letter to the book review editor of your first-choice journal. The letter should

1. Introduce you,
2. State the purpose of your correspondence,
3. Note the book that you wish to review,
4. Note previous experience, if any, and
5. Thank the editor.

In addition, you might enclose tear sheets from other reviews and a copy of your curriculum vitae. Most requests are granted.

You normally receive a complimentary copy of the book if you are solicited and agree to write the review. Sometimes the editor will provide instructions on "how to" write the review. If so, follow them exactly. If not, check recent issues. Look at the format, the structure, and the style. If there is no consistency, which is often the case, model the best reviews or use the following guidelines.

ৡৡ৶৶

A good writer is not, per se, a good book critic. No more than a good drunk is automatically a good bartender.

Jim Bishop

ৡৡ৶৶

Divide your review into three parts: (a) the title, (b) the text, and (c) author identification. Place the title at the top of the page. Divide it into two parts: the imprint matter and the description. The imprint matter includes the title of the book; the edition (if 2nd or more); the name of the author(s), compiler(s), editor(s), or translator(s); the location of the publisher; the publisher; and the year of publication. The description includes the number of pages, the list price of the book, and the International Standard Book Number (ISBN). Follow the example below:

> *Higher Education in the North.* By A. N. Snow. Whitehorse, YT: Yukon Publications, Inc., 2005. (345 pp., $80.00-hb/$40.00-pb (Cdn.), ISBN 0-1234-5678-0).

The text, like a fine journal article, should be skilfully written (see Chapters 2, 4, & 5). It needs reflection, planning, and revision, all of which enhance the final product. Keep the text between 500 and 1,000 words (two to four pages). Do not assume that the reader has read the book, direct your comments to the reader, not to the author, and discuss the book that the author wrote, not the one that they should have written.

Begin by telling the reader how you will structure the review.

State the purpose of the book. Describe the content. Summarize first. Evaluate second. Allot 70 percent of your review to evaluation. Note the positive features first; the negative features second. Do not detail small errors of fact or list obscure references that the author neglected to cite. Support your views with examples and quotations from the text. Conclude with a synopsis and a recommendation which may, or may not, be qualified.

Author identification is given immediately after the closing paragraph. It is placed to the far right and justified as shown below. It should include your name, your department, and the name of your employer.

Robin P. Norris
School of Nursing
Ryerson University

You should receive either free copies or free reprints of the journal issue. Send a copy of your review to the book publisher and one to the author(s), compiler(s), editor(s), or translator(s). Favourable reviews are usually acknowledged; unfavourable reviews are usually ignored.

Chapter Nine

Closing the Circle

What we call the beginning is often the end and to make an end is to make a beginning. The end is where we start from.

T. S. Eliot

Copyright Law

> The following material on copyright is provided solely for information purposes. The text should not be considered an authority on the topic; authority is found only in the *Copyright Act*, in the *Regulations* made under the *Act*, and in the court decisions that interpret and apply this legislation. The text thus may become outdated, in part or in whole, at any time.

*C*opyright literally means "the right to copy." The Canadian *Copyright Act* gives copyright holders the exclusive right to reproduce, to perform, or to publish a work. Specifically,

> copyright means the sole right to produce or reproduce a work or a substantial part of it in any form. It includes the right to perform the work or any substantial part of it, or in the case of a lecture, to deliver it, and if the work is unpublished, it includes the right to publish it or any substantial part of it. (Canadian Intellectual Property Office, 2005, p. 3)

In addition, copyright includes the sole right to

- produce, reproduce, perform or publish any translation of the work;
- convert a dramatic work into a novel or other non-dramatic work;
- convert a novel, a non-dramatic work or an artistic work into a dramatic work by way of performance in public or otherwise;
- make a sound recording of a literary, dramatic or musical work;
- reproduce, adapt and publicly present a cinematographic work;
- communicate the work by telecommunication;
- present an artistic work created after June 7, 1988, at a public exhibition;
- [rent out]...a computer program that can be reproduced in the ordinary course of its use...; and
- ...authorize any such acts. (pp. 3–4)

Works protected by copyright are divided into four broad categories: literary work, dramatic work, musical work, and artistic work. This summary is mainly concerned with, but not confined to, literary work. "Literary work covers everything expressed in print or writing: the form in which this occurs (paper, diskette, and the like) is irrelevant" (Vaver, 2000, p. 33). Examples include: books, computer programs, diaries, examination papers, lectures, letters (business or personal), manuals, periodicals, tables, translations, and so on. As a rule, three conditions must be satisfied for copyright to subsist in a given work.

Condition 1: *The work must be original.*

Original means that the piece must be generated by the author; it cannot be copied—it must have a modicum of creativity. The work in question does not have to be of enormous consequence. For example, an address book or a shopping list could be copyrighted if the organization of the entries is original. Thus, there is no "quality" requirement in the interpretation of the word original.

Condition 2: *The work must be an expression of an idea or fact.*

There is no copyright in ideas or facts per se, but rather in the specific words and phrases used to express the ideas or facts.

> What the law protects is the expression of these ideas [or facts]. This is based on the notion that ideas [and facts] are part of the public domain and that no one can have a monopoly in them. This basic copyright principle applies no matter how novel or great an idea [or fact]. (Harris, 2001, p. 16)

In short, it is the diction (the unique choice of words) and the syntax (the unique arrangement of words) that are protected. As such, there is usually no copyright in hackneyed historical themes or stale plots—although fresh expression of them could attract copyright. Titles have no independent protection, but original and distinctive titles are protected as part of the work in which they appear.

Condition 3: *The work must be reduced to some fixed or material form.*

Fixed means concrete, real, tangible. A handwritten, typewritten, or computer-produced paper, on disk or in hard copy, whether in point form, draft form, or polished form would be considered fixed. It is questionable, though, as to whether a transitory image on a computer screen would be protected by copyright. However, a printout of the image would be fixed and thus protected by copyright.

Copyright in Canada for published work normally lasts for the life of the author, the remainder of the calendar year in which the author dies, and 50 years thereafter. The same life-plus-fifty-year rule applies to jointly authored work, although the 50-year period begins on the death of the last living author.

Copyright protection is afforded to almost every original work in Canada. The work of an author is automatically protected under Canadian copyright law if, at the time of the creation of the work, the author was

> A a Canadian citizen or a person ordinarily resident in Canada;

> B a citizen or subject of, or a person ordinarily resident in, a Berne Convention country, a Universal Copyright Convention country, a Rome Convention country (for sound recordings, performer's performance and communication signals only), or a country that is a member of the World Trade Organization (WTO); or

> C a citizen or subject of, or a person ordinarily resident in any country

to which the Minister has extended protection by notice in the *Canada Gazette*. (Canadian Intellectual Property Office, 2005, p. 7)

As well, a work automatically has copyright if it

> was first published in one of the countries included among those who have signed the Berne, Universal Copyright or Rome Conventions or the WTO agreement, even if [the author was] not a citizen or subject of Canada, or of one of those countries. (p. 7)

Under the Berne Convention, of which most countries are members (Canada & the United States included), copyright protection arises upon creation of the work. Hence, it is not necessary to register or mark your work with a copyright notice, but its use can increase protection "in the United States since the American *Copyright Act* precludes an alleged violator from submitting that he or she did not know that copyright existed in a work where a proper copyright notice has been placed on the work" (Harris, 2001, p. 28). A copyright notice has three elements: the copyright symbol ©, the name of the copyright holder, and the year of first publication. The order is unimportant. You must, however, include all three elements. For instance, you could write the notice in one of two ways:

© Gilbert Patrick O'Neill, 2005

© 2005 by Gilbert Patrick O'Neill

Both are correct.

The author is generally the first owner of the copyright in a work. However, in the absence of an agreement to the contrary, an employer is the owner of the copyright in materials created by its employees in the course of their employment. The length of the copyright term (i.e., life plus fifty years) depends on the life of the author, not the life of the employer.

In the United States, copyright of journal articles is usually transferred to publishers by authors. In return for the publisher's agreement to publish an article, the author may be required to sign a *Copyright Transfer Form* which assigns ownership of the copyright in the article to the publisher (Day, 1998). Without a written agreement

> the publisher is presumed to have acquired only the privilege of publishing the article in the journal itself; the publisher would then lack the right to produce reprints, photocopies, and microfilms or to license others to do so (or to legally prevent others from doing so). (p. 196)

In Canada, some periodicals use assignments, others use licences. In the first case, you assign (give or sell) all or part of your economic rights permanently to the journal. In the second case, you give the journal permission to use your work, but the publisher does not own the copyright in it. A licence is like "a lease of rights" (Harris, 2001, p. 154); it is temporary and renegotiable. The standard phrase used in most contracts is, "First Canadian English-Language Serial Rights." This means the author is licensing publication of the paper one time (one-time rights) in Canada, in English, and in the journal or any periodical that publishes at regular intervals, such as a newsletter or a magazine. Each separate copyrighted use beyond the initial agreement must be negotiated with the author, who retains all other rights. At the moment, "all other rights" are unclear as they relate to electronic media. Do the rights given to a print journal, for example, extend to an electronic version of that journal? The question is presently the subject of litigation before the Supreme Court of Canada.

Most journals use a standard contract which the publisher normally presents as nonnegotiable. You either sign the agreement as presented or forego publication. Thus, you should carefully read the copyright clauses on the Author Information page before submitting your work (see Chapter 7). If the information is missing or unclear, ask the editor, particularly if you plan to use your paper later—say in an anthology. Remember, authors cannot legally duplicate their own work without permission if they have assigned their rights to that work to someone else. The Canadian *Copyright Act*

> provides that the person who receives the assignment, the assignee of rights, is treated as a copyright owner with respect to those assigned rights. The assignee may use those acquired rights in the same manner as a copyright owner, within the limitations of the agreement setting out the assignment. A full or partial assignee may also take any legal action that would be open to an owner of copyright to protect those rights. (p. 153)

As an author, however, you still retain moral rights in your work even if copyright has been transferred to another party, or belonged to an employer from its inception. Unlike economic rights, moral rights cannot be transferred to others, but they can be waived by the author. Moral rights protect the honour and reputation of the author as they relate to the creation. In other words, no one—whether an assignee (the owner) of the economic rights in copyright or anyone else—can distort, mutilate, or modify the work in such a way that it would be detrimental to the creator's good name. An assignee, for instance, cannot tamper with an author's name or pseudonym, or use the author's work in association with a product, service, cause, or institution in a manner that may be prejudicial to the author's honour or reputation without the author's consent (Vaver, 2000). This means, then, that you have some control over your work even when you created it as an employee. An employer cannot violate the author's moral rights unless, of course, the employee waives them. Moral rights can be exercised only by authors or their heirs. They last for the life of the author and for 50 years from the calendar year in which the author dies.

Obtaining Permissions

According to the Canadian *Copyright Act*, it is your responsibility to obtain permission, in writing, if you do anything with a "substantial" portion of a work which otherwise only the copyright holder has the right to do. The copyright holder need not be a person; it could be an institution. For example, in Canada, federal, provincial, and territorial government publications are covered by Crown copyright.

What is meant by "substantial" is not always clear in copyright law because there are no statutory guidelines on the number of words or phrases that may be copied and used without the copyright holder's permission. For instance, copying two lines from a small poem might be an infringement whereas copying two pages from a large book might not be, but you cannot be certain because substantiality depends on the quality as well as the quantity of the material copied. The two pages could be an infringement if, for example, they capture the essence of the book, in part, or in whole (e.g., a chapter summary).

So, how do you decide? What is substantial? What is insubstantial? The concept of *fair dealing* can help. Fair dealing allows you to copy more than an insubstantial part of a published work with impunity, provided that the work is dealt with fairly, for any of the five purposes set out in the *Act*, namely, private study, research, criticism, review, or news reporting. In cases of criticism, review, and news reporting, "both the source and the name of the author, performer, broadcaster, or sound-recording maker, if given in the source, must be mentioned before the dealing can qualify as fair" (p. 190).

Fair dealing in the Canadian *Copyright Act* allows users to disregard the claims of copyright holders if they are engaged in particular activities and meet particular conditions. To fall within the fair dealing exception for the purposes of research, you must ensure that you can show *either* (a) that your own practices and policies, or those of your institution, are research-based and fair, *or* (b) that all of your individual dealings with the materials are research-based and fair. The meaning of research is given a broad and liberal interpretation in Canadian copyright law to ensure there is no undue restriction of users' rights. If the dealing is for an allowable purpose, it must still be fair; this means that you must heed six factors.

1. *Purpose of the dealing*

   Your true purpose must be fair. The user's intentions and motives are relevant to the question of fairness. The courts, for instance, may not see research done for profit purposes (motive: to make money) to be as fair as research done for nonprofit purposes (motive: to advance knowledge).

2. *Character of the dealing*

   Character is how the user used the work. Did they make a personal copy for a particular purpose? Is the purpose listed in the *Act*? If so, the dealing may be fair. Did they make multiple copies? What did they do with them? Did they give them away (likely unfair)? Did they sell them (more likely unfair)?

3. *Amount of the dealing*

Amount depends on both the quantity and the quality of the extracts taken. Quantity is a question of degree. What is the number and extent of the extracts in relation to the entire work? As a rule, the greater the amount taken, the greater the burden of justification. At the same time, length alone does not necessarily preclude the use of a whole work. One could possibly deal fairly with an entire work provided that the owner's market is not undermined by the new work.

Quality is a question of worth. What is the significance and value of the extracts in relation to the entire work? Some parts may be more important than others. You could, for example, take two extracts of equal length from the same document. One might be considered an infringement; the other might not be considered an infringement. Much depends on the impression left with the court. Writers must take only what is reasonable for the purpose.

4. *Alternatives to the dealing*

Alternatives are works that could have been used in place of the work that was used. Was the dealing necessary? Could you have used an alternative? Was the alternative noncopyrighted? Would its use have achieved the same purpose? If so, your use of the copyrighted work may be seen as unfair.

5. *Nature of the work*

Nature means type of work. Is it published or unpublished? In general, fair dealing is harder to prove for unpublished work, especially work that was previously confidential.

6. *Impact of the work*

Impact is economic effect. What effect will a use have on the present and future market of the original work? A use that prevents a sale or reduces future sales is less likely to be seen as fair.

All six factors are used to help determine whether or not a use falls within the fair dealing exception. A use that falls within the fair dealing exception would not be an infringement of copyright. The Supreme Court of Canada has ruled that uses falling within the fair dealing exception are users' rights—not just exceptions or defences to the rights of copyright owners (*CCH Canadian Ltd.*, 2004). As a writer, you must continually ask yourself: Does my use of a copyrighted work, in sum, fall within the bounds of fair dealing? When uncertain, obtain permission from the copyright holder.

ॐॐॐॐ

Copyright is one of the most boring and complex subjects known to man.

J. G. (Jack) McClelland

ॐॐॐॐ

How do you obtain permission? Copyright for a journal article may be held by either the publisher of the journal or by the author. Write the journal and ask who owns the copyright. You can find the address on the masthead in the latest issue or in one of the periodical directories listed in Appendix H.

Books are more complex. Copyright for an authored or edited volume usually belongs to the publisher, but can be held by the author(s) or the editor(s). Check the copyright page. If there are two or more editions, you cannot assume that the same publisher holds copyright on all the editions. Earlier editions may be held by other publishers or by the author(s). This information should also be given on the copyright page. A typical disclosure might read:

Earlier editions © 2004, 1994 by Case Clark Ltd.; 1985, 1980 by Robin P. Norris.

Copyrights in an anthology may be held by the original holder of copyright in the included material as well as by the publisher of the anthology. There is copyright in the compilation that is the anthology, which the publisher of the anthology will probably hold, but which the compiler will hold before assigning it to the publisher. The compiler or publisher of the anthology may or may not have received an assignment of the copyright in the constituent works, which may have been included in the anthology simply by permission rather than by assignment of the copyright interest. You can often locate the copyright owner of the constituent works through the acknowledgment in a footnote (i.e., credit line) below the last line of text on the title page of each reprint, or in a series of endnotes on a separate page at the end of the volume. A typical credit line might read:

> Reprinted from..., by permission of the publisher and the author. (Copyright, 1942, by...).

Use of a translation may require permission from the translator or the publisher of the translation as well as from the author or publisher of the original work. Check the copyright page to see if the original work is still under copyright.

The publishing industry has changed greatly in the last decade. Many companies have been restructured, merged, or sold. As a result, the publisher's address in older editions may be incorrect. It is best, therefore, to confirm the current mailing address in one of the publisher directories listed in Appendix H before sending a request.

A typical letter requesting permission to use copyrighted material is given in Figure 9-1. Send your request to either the permissions department or the editorial director (editor-in-chief) who will channel it to the person responsible. Begin by stating your purpose. Then, give the source from which you wish to quote. Give the author, the year of publication, the title, the location of the publisher, and the publisher. Include a description of any changes that you plan to make in the material (e.g., an abridgement).

If you are requesting permission to use copyrighted material in a book you are writing, ask for world rights in English and in any translated volumes. State the approximate length of your book, the projected publication date, the estimated retail price, and the type of edition (hardback, paperback, or both). Ask for permission that will cover all future editions.

June 15, 2005

N. Big Canoe, Editor-in-Chief
Yukon Publications, Inc.
7 Polar Bear Pl.
Whitehorse, YT A1B 2C3

Dear N. Big Canoe:

I am writing a paper entitled, "In Defence of the Doctoral Dissertation." As part of the text, I would like to get permission to use part of Table 9 which appears on page 242 in: Snow, A. N. (2005). *Higher Education in the North*. Whitehorse, YT: Yukon Publications, Inc. Do I also need the author's permission? If so, please provide me with the latest address.

The credit line will read as follows:
        From *Higher Education in the North* (p. 242) by A. N. Snow. Copyright © 2005 by Yukon Publications Inc. Reprinted by (with) permission of (from) Yukon Publications, Inc., Whitehorse, YT and A. N. Snow (if applicable).
Is this satisfactory? If not, please specify the credit line you prefer.

_____
_____
_____

I plan to submit my manuscript for publication in November, 2005. I would, therefore, appreciate a response by *October, 2005*.

If you agree to the above use, please sign the form below and return one signed copy of this letter to me in the enclosed, self-addressed, stamped envelope. Retain the second copy for your records.

Yours truly,

G. Patrick O'Neill, Ph.D.
Attached (1)

We hereby grant permission for _____ to use the material as specified in this letter.

_____

Name (type or print) for Yukon Publishers, Inc.

_____   _____
Signature   Date

Figure 9-1. An example of a permissions letter.

Next, ask if you need the author's permission. If so, ask for the address. Then, state how you will acknowledge the material and ask whether, or not, it is satisfactory. End by specifying a return date; ask the publisher to sign the form if they agree to the request, and ask them to return one signed copy of the letter in the return, self-addressed, stamped envelope. Use International Reply Coupons for return postage if you are sending your requests outside Canada. Send two copies of everything. Staple copies of the page(s) in question to the cover letter and bracket in red ink the sections that you wish to borrow. Always give the publisher sufficient lead time (at least 2 months) to consider your request. Keep a record of all your correspondence.

If your request is granted, keep the letter or a copy of the letter in your files. You will be asked to share the originals with your publisher. If your request is denied, you have three options: drop the section, bring its use within the bounds of fair dealing, or replace it with other material.

Sometimes, the granting of permission will hinge on a fee. The amount will depend on the number and extent of the extracts. Fees are negotiable. Get a receipt if you pay a fee.

Collaborative Authorship

৵৵৵৵

Remember upon the conduct of each depends the fate of all.

Alexander the Great

৵৵৵৵

Three factors have contributed to an increase in collaborative authorships: the "publish or perish" edict, joint efforts by graduate students and their supervisors, and the complexity of research projects themselves (Norris, 1993). Collaboration is defined as two or more people working together to produce a literary work.

Collaboration "can result in a better product,...it is in certain situations the only way to get a large-scale project accomplished,... [and] it enhances possibilities for achieving less fragmented bodies of knowledge through interdisciplinary cooperation" (Ashton-Jones, 1997, p. 189). At the same time, however, the practice is "rife with possibilities for conflict" (p. 184). How do you define authorship? Who gets first authorship, second authorship, and so forth? How do you decide? When do you decide? How do you write bylines? Answers to these questions need to be fully addressed and clearly understood before entering into any collaborative contract.

How do you define authorship? Unfortunately, there is no standard definition of authorship (Luey, 2002). Nonetheless, most definitions "revolve around two issues: knowledge and responsibility" (p. 17). Phrases such as "intellectual responsibility" (Day, 1998, p. 24), "responsibility and content" (Huth, 1999, p. 42), and "public responsibility" (National Research Council of Canada, 1993, p. 275) suggest the ability to "defend" the work should it be challenged by others. You can defend the work only if you understand the work, and you can understand the work only if you are actively involved in "all" aspects of the work.

Those who perform "only" mechanical, procedural, and technical functions are excluded from this definition. Excluded are

1. Those who conducted literature searches,
2. Those who gave permission for the study,
3. Those who administered surveys, interviewed participants, or tested subjects,
4. Those who inputted data,
5. Those who developed computer programs,
6. Those who ran data analyses,
7. Those who computer-produced the manuscript,
8. Those who proofed the text for typographical errors,
9. Those who helped arrange for the working space, equipment, and so on,
10. Those who contributed financial support.

How do you decide the order of authorship? Ideally, the order should depend on the "scholarly importance" of each contribution. Importance should not be defined by the amount of time and effort expended, or by the power structure of the team. Rather, it should depend on the overall contribution of each member. There are four areas in which each member is expected to participate, but the degree of participation may vary. The four areas are

1. Designing (planning and organizing the project),
2. Developing (collecting, analyzing, and interpreting the data),
3. Drafting (writing, revising, and editing the text),
4. Defending (answering queries, reading reviews, and preparing rebuttals).

The first, or principal, author might be the person who makes a major contribution in all four areas. The second author might be the person who makes a major contribution in three of the areas and a minor contribution in one of the areas. The third author might be the person who makes a major and a minor contribution in each of two areas. The fourth author might be the person who makes a major contribution in one area and a minor contribution in three areas. The fifth author might be the person who makes a minor contribution in all four areas.

The principal author is usually the coordinator of the project. They are responsible for scheduling meetings, setting deadlines, ensuring consistency in style and format, resolving minor disputes, and handling all correspondence.

When should you decide on the order of authorship? As a rule, the order should be decided in advance. It is strongly recommended that you put your agreement in writing as people sometimes forget. Jockeying for the primary position after the fact can lead to resentment and petty reprisals that could later damage your career, especially if you are vulnerable (i.e., nontenured).

> I haven't yet heard of a duel being fought over the order of listing of authors, but I know of instances in which otherwise reasonable, rational colleagues have become bitter enemies solely because they could not agree on whose names should be listed or in what order. (Day, 1998, p. 22)

Once the order has been established and agreed upon

> the authors-to-be can then decide on how to divide the work of writing

the paper. With relatively short papers the first draft is probably best written by only one author, but with long and complex papers the work may be shared to advantage. For example, the sections on study design and statistical analysis in a paper reporting a large cooperative study are probably best written by its statistician. With such division of work on early drafts, agreement should also be reached on their deadlines and who will pull them together for a single, integrated manuscript. (Huth, 1999, p. 45)

Sometimes, the relative contributions change. If this happens, you will have to renegotiate your position. As a result, your name could be

1. Moved forward or backward,
2. Reduced to an acknowledgement, or
3. Removed.

If disputes arise, let an impartial arbitrator settle the matter.

How do you write bylines? Bylines should reflect the order of authorship. That is, the principal contributor should be listed in the first position, the second contributor in the second position, and the like. But, what is the first position? Again, there is no consensus. "Conventions differ between and within disciplines" (Harsanyi, 1993, p. 338). Thus, you have two choices. You can either follow the accepted conventions of your discipline (if there are any) or explain the order in a footnote. There are six basic ways to write bylines:

1. List the principal author first; other authors are then listed in order of decreasing importance (X, 1 2 3).
2. List the principal author first; other authors are then listed in alphabetical order (X, ABC).
3. List the principal author last; other authors are then listed, from first to last, in order of decreasing importance (1 2 3, X).
4. List the principal author last; other authors are then listed, from first to last, in alphabetical order (ABC, X).
5. List all the names in alphabetical order when the contributions are deemed equal (ABCD).
6. Rotate the names, in a series, so that everyone has the opportunity of being listed in the first position (1 2 3 4; 2 3 4 1; 3 4 1 2; 4 1 2 3).

The issue is not as crucial with coauthorships because you can reverse the names from publication to publication. If there is only one publication, however, and you are an established scholar, you might consider giving the first position to a younger colleague. This noble practice encourages the next generation, promotes the ethic of "fair play," and enhances the reputation of those who engage in it.

ॐॐॐॐ

There are two classes, those who want to know and do not care whether others think they know or not, and those who do not much care about knowing but care very greatly about being reputed as knowing.

Samuel Butler

ॐॐॐॐ

Professional Ethics

Ethics are defined as the rules or standards governing the proper conduct of the members of a profession, in this case academics. Acts of misconduct can be classified as immoral or illegal, or both. The phrase "or both" is used because moral positions can have legal implications just as legal positions can be morally damaging. For instance, misrepresenting yourself (a moral infraction) through false authorships and distorted autobiographical notes, could be grounds for legal action, particularly if the information was knowingly used to beguile an employer in the areas of promotion, tenure, merit pay, salary increments, and so on. The point is, the two are not necessarily inseparable.

Moral Misconduct

Moral misconduct includes (a) fabrication, (b) falsification, (c) fragmentation, (d) duplicate publication, (e) gratuitous authorship, (f) multiple submission, (g) dishonest reviews, and (h) public misrepresentation. *Fabrication* is forging or making up data. It goes by the nickname "drylabbing." *Falsification* is changing or manipulating findings until they "fit" the author's preconceived premise. It is commonly known as "cooking", "fudging", or "massaging" the data. *Fragmentation* is splintered reporting; breaking data into the greatest number of least publishable units (LPUs). It is known in the industry as "salami publication." It is a disreputable practice because it unduly overloads the review process, it clutters the literature with scraps of information, it fragments electronic abstract-retrieval systems, and it artificially inflates the reputation of the author(s).

Duplicate publication is defined as

> not only [the] exact duplication of a paper (exactly the same title, abstract, text, references, tables, and illustrations) but also [the] repeated publication of essentially the same information whether or not it is presented in precisely the same way. (Huth, 1990, pp. 186–187)

In effect, the author recycles old material disguised as new material. Morgan (1983) identified four types of duplicators: the pyramid builders, the Januses, the manipulators, and the desperadoes. Pyramid builders are those who publish a series of releases from the same project. Each piece is a rerun except for one small addition. They believe "that each article should be a picture of the entire pyramid as it is being built, not just one brick" (p. 240). The Januses speak to two audiences at the same time by repeatedly publishing a slightly different version of the same manuscript in closely related fields. The manipulators send their articles simultaneously to several journals "intending to withdraw the others when one is accepted. Sometimes they 'forget' to withdraw the papers in time and thus become the final and most blatant duplicators, the desperadoes" (p. 240). Duplicate publication is acceptable only when

1. The editors of both works are fully informed.
2. Copyright laws are not violated.
3. The author discloses the primary publication in a footnote.
4. The secondary version is published after the primary version.

Work that meets these four conditions may be republished in

1. A collected reprints volume,
2. An edited book of readings,
3. A foreign language periodical,
4. A foreign language book.

Gratuitous authorship, sometimes called honorary authorship, is false authorship. It is the clandestine

> practice whereby persons not wholly accountable for the work have their names affixed to publications with motives to increase the bibliographies of a number of persons and sometimes, to create the impression of a luminary (though nominal) contributor to the publication. (Fox, 1994, p. 301)

Gratuitous authorship is unethical because it is assumed that the work listed in your bibliography is your work, not that of others. If this is untrue, then the question becomes: Whose work is it? Gratuitous listings are fraudulent listings. And fraudulent listings make a mockery of a profession that is supposedly committed to the pursuit of truth.

> If the author is not really the author, not really responsible for the article's success or failure, then the entire relationship [between the editor and author] collapses. Authorship appears to be a sham and, like the Cheshire cat, disappears before our eyes in a fog of dishonesty and mocking deceit. (LaFollette, 1992, p. 106)

Multiple submission is the act of simultaneously submitting the same manuscript to two or more journals without notifying the editors. It is unethical because the perpetrator must withdraw the paper from the other publishers once an acceptance is received, or risk a charge of duplicate publication. Understandably, editors loathe the practice because it overloads the system with needless reviews, thereby wasting their time and the reviewers' time. Repeated offenders could get a bad reputation; one that bars them from any further publication in reputable journals.

Dishonest reviews arise when referees fail to disclose their knowledge limitations, their personal relationships, and their extreme academic biases. Knowledge limitations restrict the topics which reviewers can adequately assess. They "should serve only in their areas of expertise. A referee who feels inadequately qualified to evaluate a manuscript should return it promptly to the Editor" (National Research Council of Canada, 1993, p. 277).

Personal relationships should not interfere with the review process. A referee who "inappropriately praises the manuscript of a friend, former student, or mentor without revealing the relationship deceives the editor" (LaFollette, 1992, p. 55). All reviews must be kept at arm's length.

Extreme academic biases can hinder the review process, especially in situations where the reviewer and the reviewee are "intellectual" rivals. A referee, for instance, could wittingly "discredit" a finding or a theory knowing very well that their comments will stall or stop the publication (p. 55). Reviewers have a moral obligation to declare their extreme biases (negative or positive) at the outset, and decline the review.

Public misrepresentation is the deliberate distortion of words with the intent to create a false, positive impression. It is found in general statements like: "The author has published three books." The term "published" is ambiguous. It can be interpreted to mean

1. The author wrote some or all of the books.
2. The author compiled some or all of the books.
3. The author edited some or all of the books.
4. The author translated some or all of the books.
5. The author published some or all of the books.

Why did this person pick the word published? Was it to impress the readership? Will most readers assume, unsuspectingly, that the person wrote the books when, in fact, they were edited? Was this the intent? If so, the word "published" is used, in this context, as a weasel word. A weasel word is a word intentionally used to mislead the reader. A specific statement will clarify the matter. Say: "The author has coedited three books." Or, better still, "The author has coedited three college textbooks."

The word published literally means "to prepare and issue the work of an author." This means, then, that in this case, the person prepared and issued their own work. There are only two ways to do this, self-publication and vanity presses, neither of which carries any prestige in academe.

જ્જજ્જ

How often misused words generate misleading thoughts.

Herbert Spencer

જ્જજ્જ

Legal Misconduct

Legal misconduct includes plagiarism and pilfering. *Plagiarism* is claiming the words or phrases of another person as your own. There are blatant and subtle forms of plagiarism. A blatant example would be the verbatim republishing of another person's work "almost in toto" (LaFollette, 1992, p. 50) without acknowledging the author and getting permission from the copyright holder, whether the author or their assignee. Subtle plagiarism is harder to detect because it can be "a mixture of original text and rephrasing, perhaps with attribution, without quotation marks, and with the implication that the phrasings and interpretation are the plagiarist's own" (p. 49). Those who plagiarize the work of others risk eventual detection, professional and public disgrace, academic sanctions, dismissal from employment, and the awarding of damages under the *Copyright Act*.

Pilfering is taking and exploiting the unpublished work of colleagues or subordinates, or both. It is inappropriate, for example, for referees to copy or republish material from manuscripts that they have been entrusted to review. The practice is "universally condemned" because it "breaks the relationship of trust on which the peer review process depends" (p. 56). A referee who pilfers could be sued for breach of confidence.

Likewise, a supervisor cannot publish material from a student's thesis or dissertation without the student's consent. The copyright and moral rights in the thesis or dissertation belong to the student. Moreover, a faculty member cannot take authorship credit that is earned by a student. The student is normally listed as the first author on any joint publication that is based primarily on the student's thesis or dissertation, although a student might decline first authorship in situations where the faculty member takes "responsibility" for writing and revising most of the manuscript.

Loose Ends

This section contains 17 questions and 17 answers on subjects that have not been fully addressed in the preceding text. The objective is to help clarify issues and terms that are often misunderstood by both aspiring and established authors.

Question 1:   *May you write a paper from a thesis or dissertation before it is finished?*

As a rule, you may, but it is best to check with your supervisor before proceeding because disciplines vary somewhat; some encourage the practice, others discourage the practice.

Question 2:   *Will a book publisher publish a dissertation if you have published papers from it?*

Yes, most will consider it for publication provided that not more than 20 to 30 percent is prepublished. It is the author's responsibility, however, to ensure that copyright laws are not violated.

Question 3:   *Is it ethical to present a paper at a conference and then submit it to a journal for publication?*

The practice is ethical, provided that the paper is not published as part of the conference proceedings. If it is, then a second publication could be deemed duplicate publication.

Question 4:   *Is duplicate presentation the same as duplicate publication?*

Yes, it is. Repeated presentation of basically the same paper, whether it is exactly the same or slightly altered, without full disclosure, is unethical. You must note previous presentations in either a footnote or an endnote. You cannot present old material as new material.

Question 5:   *Is it ethical to use the same material in both a poster presentation and in a journal article?*

In general, it is, provided that the poster presentation is done first. Posters are classified as preliminary reports, that is, abstracts or summaries. Therefore, they do not preclude a journal article. The article would serve a different purpose, take a different form, and target a different audience.

Question 6:   *Is it ethical to send a query letter to more than one journal at a time?*

Yes, provided that you are forthright. You must stress that you are conducting a preliminary poll, that you are scouting for possible outlets, and that a final submission-decision will be made once the manuscript is finished. In short, you are not making any commitments at this stage, you are only gathering information. Multiple submission of your final manuscript, however, is unethical.

Question 7:   *What are tear sheets?*

Tear sheets are pages taken from a periodical to help illustrate the quality of your work. They are often used with query letters.

Question 8:   *What does the phrase in progress mean?*

In progress means that you are working on a document. It could be in different stages: outline, first draft, final draft. The work may be listed in your bibliography as "in progress", but it should never be listed as a source in a reference list, or counted as a publication.

Question 9:   *What does the word pending mean?*

Pending means that a manuscript is under review. It has been submitted for publication, but no decision has been made as to whether or not it will be published. It could be in either the initial stages of the review process or it could have been sent back, revised, and resubmitted for further review. It may be listed in your bibliography as "pending" and it may be cited in other work and in your reference list as an unpublished manuscript, but it cannot be counted as a publication.

Question 10:   *What does the phrase in press mean?*

In press means that a manuscript has been "unconditionally" accepted for publication. It has been submitted, reviewed, revised, edited, and is now in the production phase. A paper accepted for publication, but not yet published may be

1. Listed in your bibliography as (in press),
2. Cited in other work and in your reference list as (in press),
3. Counted as a publication.

Question 11:   *What does the word prestige mean?*

Prestige is synonymous with academic reputation. The greater your reputation, the greater your prestige. Reputation is based mainly on your scholarly productivity. And productivity is measured primarily by refereed journal articles (see Chapter 7) and peer-reviewed books (see Chapter 8). Prestige among journals is determined by rejection rates. The higher the rejection rate, the greater is the journal's prestige, thus the phrase "prestigious journal." Prestige among books is determined by five factors:

1. The type of text (authored, compiled, edited, translated),
2. The type of book (scholarly, text, trade),
3. The type of publisher (university, societal, commercial scholarly, textbook, trade, vanity),
4. The size of the press, and
5. The age of the press.

The most prestigious combination would probably be an authored, scholarly book published by a large, established university press. It is the most prestigious combination because generally

1. Authored books have more prestige than compiled, edited, or translated books.
2. Scholarly books have more prestige than either textbooks or trade books.
3. University presses have more prestige than other types of presses.

4. Larger presses have more prestige than smaller presses, and

5. Older presses have more prestige than newer presses.

The least prestigious combination would be a compiled or edited trade book published by a vanity press. Other combinations would fall between the two. For instance, a translated scholarly book published by a small, established societal press might have more prestige than an edited scholarly book published by a large, commercial scholarly press (old or new). The point is, there is far more subjectivity involved in assessing book prestige than in assessing journal prestige. Hence,

> book chapters, books, monographs, book reviews, and the like are useful scholarly contributions but in general are accorded neither the attention nor the value ascribed to journal articles. (Thyer, 1994, p. 9)

༺༠༚༚

It is with books as with men: a very small number play a great part, the rest are lost in the multitude.
Voltaire

༺༠༚༚

Question 12:   *What is a peer-reviewed journal?*

A *peer-reviewed* journal, sometimes called a juried journal, is one that reviews its manuscripts prior to publication. The reviews are done by a panel of peers, thus the phrase "peer-reviewed." There are two types of reviews, open and closed (see Chapter 7). An open review is one in which the author's identity is known to the reviewers. In contrast, a closed review conceals the author's identity from the reviewers, but not necessarily the reviewers from the author.

> Opinions differ on whether reviewers should remain anonymous. Some editors require their reviewers to sign the comments returned to authors, but most either request that reviewers' comments not be signed or leave the choice to the reviewer. When comments are not signed the reviewers' identity must not be revealed to the author or anyone else. (Huth, 1999, p. 311)

This type of review is called a *blind review*. Blind-reviewed journals are refereed journals. Occasionally, the phrase double-blind review is used. It is *double-blind* because neither are the authors disclosed to the reviewers nor the reviewers to the authors. All correspondence is masked. Sometimes journals use double-blind review, but call it blind review.

Question 13: *Is a journal a periodical?*

Yes, a journal is a periodical, but a periodical is not necessarily a journal. The word *periodical* encompasses the terms bulletin, journal, magazine, newsletter, and pamphlet. A *bulletin* is defined as

> a publication, generally a pamphlet, issued by a government, society or other organization at regular intervals and in serial form. (Prytherch, 2000, p. 108)

A *journal* is defined as

> a periodical, especially one containing scholarly articles and/or disseminating current information on research and development in a particular subject field. (Young, 1983, p. 125)

A *magazine* is defined as

> a periodical for general reading containing articles on various subjects by different authors. (p. 137)

A *newsletter* is defined as

> a serial consisting of one or a few printed sheets containing news or information of interest chiefly to a special group. (p. 153)

A *pamphlet* is defined as

> an independent publication consisting of a few leaves of printed matter fastened together but not bound; usually enclosed in paper covers. Also called a brochure. (p. 162)

Question 14: *What is a monograph?*

A *monograph* is a small book. It is a bound volume containing a detailed, documented treatise on a particular subject within a field of study. It can be a single volume or several volumes in a series. Each volume would be a special account of a single subject.

Question 15: *What does the word exploit mean?*

The term is a copyright concept. It means that an author has the right to sell their rights to a work in exchange for money. There are a *bundle* of rights attached to a work. They include publication, reproduction, translation, and so forth. As the author, you have the right to exploit these rights and be monetarily compensated for the exploitation. For example, you could sign a book contract in exchange for royalties. You could sell all your rights to one publisher or divide them among many publishers for different lengths of time in specific countries or worldwide. Simply put, you have full control over how, when, and where your work is used, and you can exploit those uses to your advantage.

Question 16: *What is the difference between an acronym and an initialism?*

Both are abbreviations formed from the initial letters of a compound word, but they are pronounced differently. An *acronym* is a "letter group that can be, and is, pronounced as a word: NATO..." (McArthur, 1992, p. 3). An *initialism* is "a letter group that cannot be pronounced as a word, and must therefore be spoken as letters: BBC..." (p. 3). CD-ROM (compact disc read-only memory) is part initialism and part acronym.

Question 17: *What is the difference between a primary and a secondary source?*

Primary sources are full-text documents that contain firsthand literary works and original research reports. The information is communicated directly from the author to the reader; there is no intermediary. In contrast, *secondary* sources are at least once removed from the initial record. They contain secondhand literary accounts (summaries and translations) and research reviews in which the work of others is critiqued, described, explained, or interpreted. The information is communicated indirectly from the author to the reader via an intermediary. The intermediary could be an abstracter, a book reviewer, a commentator, a critic, or a translator. The original writings of Jean-Jacques Rousseau, for instance, are primary sources (e.g., *Emile*), whereas contemporary reviews of his work would be considered secondary sources. Primary sources include articles in primary periodicals, theses and dissertations, government reports, private and public agency reports, scholarly books and monographs, and the like. Secondary sources include articles in review periodicals (e.g., *Harvard Educational Review*), book reviews, subject reviews (e.g., *Encyclopedia of Mental Health*), textbooks, yearbooks (e.g., *The Europa World Year Book*), and so on.

Clarity, clarity, clarity.

E. B. White

I see but one rule: to be clear.

Stendhal

There is no Heaven but clarity, no
Hell except confusion.

Jan Struther

Appendix A

A List of 420 Canadian Periodicals

Note 1. This is not an exhaustive list.

Note 2. The list includes print periodicals, electronic periodicals, and print and electronic periodicals.

Note 3. The list is divided into 50 categories: 49 specific categories and 1 International category. The International category contains periodicals that are produced in part by organizations both inside and outside Canada.

Note 4. The categories and the titles within categories are in alphabetical order with no inversions for titles that begin with abbreviations.

Note 5. The article "the" is omitted at the beginning of all titles. For instance, *The Canadian Geographer* is listed as *Canadian Geographer/Géographe canadien*.

Note 6. Interdisciplinary periodicals can be placed in two or more categories, but here they are not. For example, the *Education & Law Journal/Revue de droit de l'éducation* is placed in the Education category.

Categories

Aeronautics and Space
Agriculture
Anthropology
Archaeology
Architecture
Art
Biological Sciences
Business and Economics
Chemistry
Classical Studies
Communication and
    Journalism Studies
Computer Science
Criminology
Dentistry
Earth Sciences
Education
Engineering

Environmental Studies
Ethnic and Cultural Studies
Film
Food and Nutrition
Geography
Gerontology
Health Sciences
History
International
Labour Studies
Language and Linguistics
Law
Library and
    Information Studies
Literature
Mathematics and Statistics
Medicine
Music

Native Studies
Nursing
Pharmacology
Philosophy
Physics
Political Science
Population Studies
Psychology
Public Administration
Recreation and
    Leisure Studies
Religious Studies
Social Work
Sociology
Theatre
Veterinary Medicine
Women's Studies

Aeronautics and Space
Annals of Air and Space Law / Annales de droit aérien et spatial
Canadian Aeronautics and Space Journal / Journal aéronautique et spatial du Canada
Canadian Journal of Remote Sensing / Journal canadien de télédétection
Journal of the Royal Astronomical Society of Canada / Journal de la Société royale d'astronomie du Canada

Agriculture
Canadian Journal of Agricultural Economics / Revue canadienne d'agroeconomie
Canadian Journal of Animal Science / Revue canadienne de zootechnie
Canadian Journal of Plant Science / Revue canadienne de phytotechnie
Canadian Journal of Soil Science / Revue canadienne de la science du sol
Current Agriculture, Food and Resource Issues

Anthropology
Anthropologica
Anthropologie et sociétés
Ethnologies
Nexus: Canadian Student Journal of Anthropology / Journal des étudiants canadiens en anthropologie

Archaeology
Canadian Journal of Archaeology / Journal canadien d'archéologie
Manitoba Archaeological Journal
Ontario Archaeology

Architecture
Canadian Architect
Journal of the Society for the Study of Architecture in Canada / Journal de la Société pour l'étude de l'architecture au Canada

Art
Canadian Art Teacher / Enseigner les arts au Canada
Canadian Review of Art Education: Research and Issues / Revue canadienne d'éducation artistique: recherche et questions d'actualité artistique
Journal of Canadian Art History / Annales d'histoire de l'art canadien
Parachute
RACAR: revue d'art canadienne / Canadian Art Review

Biological Sciences
    Archaea: An International Microbiological Journal
    Biochemistry and Cell Biology / Biochimie et biologie cellulaire
    Canadian Entomologist
    Canadian Field-Naturalist
    Canadian Journal of Botany / Revue canadienne de botanique
    Canadian Journal of Fisheries and Aquatic Sciences / Journal canadien des sciences halieutiques et aquatiques
    Canadian Journal of Forest Research / Revue canadienne de recherche forestière
    Canadian Journal of Microbiology / Revue canadienne de microbiologie
    Canadian Journal of Physiology and Pharmacology / Revue canadienne de physiologie et pharmacologie
    Canadian Journal of Plant Pathology / Revue canadienne de phytopathologie
    Canadian Journal of Zoology / Revue canadienne de zoologie
    Forestry Chronicle
    Genome / Génome
    Journal of Northwest Atlantic Fishery Science
    Phytoprotection

Business and Economics
    Canadian Accounting Perspectives / Perspectives comptables canadiennes
    Canadian Journal of Administrative Sciences / Revue canadienne des sciences de l'administration
    Canadian Journal of Development Studies / Revue canadienne d'études du développement
    Canadian Journal of Economics / Revue canadienne d'économique
    Canadian Public Policy / Analyse de politiques
    Canadian Tax Journal / Revue fiscale canadienne
    Contemporary Accounting Research / Recherche comptable contemporaine
    International Journal of Arts Management
    JKMP: Journal of Knowledge Management Practice
    Journal of Accounting Case Research
    Journal of Comparative International Management
    JSBE: Journal of Small Business & Entrepreneurship
    Studies in Political Economy: A Socialist Review

Chemistry
    Canadian Journal of Analytical Sciences and Spectroscopy
    Canadian Journal of Chemistry / Revue canadienne de chimie
    Clinical Biochemistry

Classical Studies
Mouseion: Journal of the Classical Association of Canada / Revue de la Société canadienne des études classiques
Phoenix

Communication and Journalism Studies
Canadian Journal of Communication
Communication: information, médias, théories, pratiques
Journal of Scholarly Publishing
Technostyle: Journal of the Canadian Teachers of Technical Writing

Computer Science
Control and Intelligent Systems
INFOR: Information Systems and Operational Research / Systèmes d'information et recherche opérationnelle
International Journal of Robotics and Automation

Criminology
Canadian Journal of Criminology and Criminal Justice / Revue canadienne de criminologie et de justice pénale
Canadian Society of Forensic Science Journal / Journal de la Société canadienne des sciences judiciaires
Criminologie

Dentistry
Canadian Journal of Dental Hygiene
JCDA / JADC: Journal of the Canadian Dental Association / Journal de l'Association dentaire canadienne
Oral Health

Earth Sciences
Atlantic Geology: Journal of the Atlantic Geoscience Society / Revue de la Société géoscientifique de l'Atlantique
Atmosphere-Ocean
Canadian Geotechnical Journal / Revue canadienne de géotechnique
Canadian Journal of Earth Sciences / Revue canadienne des sciences de la terre
Canadian Metallurgical Quarterly
Canadian Minerologist
Exploration and Mining Geology: Journal of the Geological Society of CIM
Geomatica
Geoscience Canada
JCPT: Journal of Canadian Petroleum Technology

Education
    Alberta Journal of Educational Research
    Canadian and International Education/Éducation canadienne et internationale
    Canadian Children: Journal of the Canadian Association for Young Children
    Canadian Journal for the Study of Adult Education/Revue canadienne pour
        l'étude de l'éducation des adultes
    Canadian Journal of Education/Revue canadienne de l'éducation
    Canadian Journal of Educational Administration and Policy
    Canadian Journal of Environmental Education
    Canadian Journal of Higher Education/Revue canadienne d'enseignement
        supérieur
    Canadian Journal of Learning and Technology/Revue canadienne de
        l'apprentissage et de la technologie
    Canadian Journal of School Psychology
    Canadian Journal of Science, Mathematics and Technology Education/Revue
        canadienne de l'enseignement des sciences, des mathématiques et des
        technologies
    Canadian Journal of University Continuing Education/Revue canadienne de
        l'éducation permanente universitaire
    Canadian Social Studies
    College Quarterly
    Curriculum Inquiry
    EAF Journal: Journal of Educational Administration and Foundations
    Early Childhood Education
    Education & Law Journal/Revue de droit de l'éducation
    Education Canada
    English Quarterly
    Exceptionality Education Canada
    Historical Studies in Education/Revue d'histoire de l'éducation
    IEJLL: International Electronic Journal for Leadership in Learning
    Interchange
    International Review of Research in Open and Distance Learning
    JET: Journal of Educational Thought/Revue de la pensée éducative
    Journal of Distance Education/Revue de l'éducation à distance
    Language & Literacy: A Canadian Educational E-Journal
    McGill Journal of Education/Revue des sciences de l'éducation de McGill
    Paideusis: Journal of the Canadian Philosophy of Education Society
    Policy and Practice in Education
    TESL Canada Journal/Revue TESL du Canada

Engineering
> *Canadian Biosystems Engineering / Génie des biosystèmes au Canada*
> *Canadian Journal of Chemical Engineering*
> *Canadian Journal of Civil Engineering / Revue canadienne de génie civil*
> *Canadian Journal of Electrical and Computer Engineering / Revue canadienne*
>   *de génie électrique et informatique*
> *International Journal of Chemical Reactor Engineering*
> *International Journal of Forest Engineering*
> *Journal of Environmental Engineering and Science / Revue du génie et de la*
>   *science de l'environnement*
> *Journal of Pulp and Paper Science*

Environmental Studies
> *Biodiversity*
> *Canadian Journal of Regional Science / Revue canadienne des sciences régionales*
> *Canadian Journal of Urban Research / Revue canadienne de recherche urbaine*
> *Canadian Water Resources Journal / Revue canadienne des ressources hydriques*
> *Écoscience*
> *Energy Studies Review*
> *Environmental Reviews / Dossiers environnement*
> *Environments*
> *Journal of Great Lakes Research*
> *Plan Canada*
> *Prairie Forum*
> *Water Quality Research Journal of Canada*

Ethnic and Cultural Studies
> *B.C. Asian Review*
> *BC Studies: British Columbian Quarterly*
> *Canadian Ethnic Studies / Études ethniques au Canada*
> *Canadian Jewish Studies / Études juives canadiennes*
> *Canadian Journal of African Studies / Revue canadienne des études africaines*
> *Canadian Journal of Irish Studies / Revue canadienne d'études irlandaises*
> *Canadian Journal of Latin American and Caribbean Studies / Revue*
>   *canadienne des études latino-américaines et caraïbes*
> *Canadian Slavonic Papers / Revue canadienne des slavistes*
> *Interculture*
> *International Journal of Canadian Studies / Revue internationale d'études canadiennes*
> *Journal of Canadian Studies / Revue d'études canadiennes*
> *Journal of Ukrainian Studies*
> *Newfoundland Studies*
> *Scandinavian-Canadian Studies / Études scandinaves au Canada*
> *Seminar: A Journal of Germanic Studies*
> *Topia: Canadian Journal of Cultural Studies*

Film
Canadian Journal of Film Studies / Revue canadienne d'études
cinématographiques
Cineaction
Kinema: A Journal for Film and Audiovisual Media

Food and Nutrition
Canadian Journal of Dietetic Practice and Research / Revue canadienne de la
pratique et de la recherche en diététique
Food Research International

Geography
Arctic
Cahiers de géographie du Québec
Canadian Geographer / Géographe canadien
Cartographica
Géographie physique et quaternaire

Gerontology
Canadian Journal on Aging / Revue canadienne du vieillissement
Geriatrics & Aging
Perspectives: Journal of the Gerontological Nursing Association

Health Sciences
Canadian Journal of Diabetes
Canadian Journal of Infection Control / Revue canadienne de prévention des infections
Canadian Journal of Medical Radiation Technology / Journal canadien des
technologies en radiation médicale
Canadian Journal of Occupational Therapy / Revue canadienne d'ergothérapie
Canadian Journal of Optometry / Revue canadienne d'optométrie
Canadian Journal of Public Health / Revue canadienne de santé publique
Chronic Diseases in Canada
CJRT / RCTR: Canadian Journal of Respiratory Therapy / Revue canadienne de
la thérapie respiratoire
Healthcare Management Forum / Forum gestion des soins de santé
International Journal of Disability, Community & Rehabilitation
International Journal of Forensic Mental Health
Journal of Palliative Care
Journal of the Canadian Chiropractic Association / Journal de l'Association
chiropratique canadienne
Journal on Developmental Disabilities / Journal sur les handicaps du développement
JSLPA / ROA: Journal of Speech-Language Pathology and Audiology / Revue
d'orthophonie et d'audiologie
Physiotherapy Canada / Physiothérapie Canada

History

Acadiensis: Journal of the History of the Atlantic Region / Revue de l'histoire de la région Atlantique

Archivaria

Canadian Historical Review

Canadian Journal of History / Annales canadiennes d'histoire

Canadian Review of American Studies

Canadian Review of Studies in Nationalism / Revue canadienne des études sur le nationalisme

History of Intellectual Culture

International History Review

International Journal of Maritime History

Journal of the Canadian Historical Association / Revue de la Société historique du Canada

Manitoba History

Material History Review / Revue d'histoire de la culture matérielle

Northern Mariner / Marin du nord

Ontario History

Oral History Forum / Forum d'histoire orale

Scientia Canadensis: Journal of the History of Canadian Science, Technology and Medicine / Revue d'histoire des sciences, des techniques et de la médecine au Canada

Urban History Review / Revue d'histoire urbaine

International

Biotechnology Advances

Children's Literature in Education: An International Quarterly

Clinical Journal of Sport Medicine

Clinical Nursing Research

Ecology and Society

Electronic Journal of Computational Kinematics

Evolution and Human Behaviour

Journal of Advanced Oxidation Technologies

Journal of Sport Management

Journal of Toxicology and Environmental Health Part A: Current Issues

Journal of Toxicology and Environmental Health Part B: Critical Reviews

Qualitative Health Research: An International, Interdisciplinary Journal

Transcultural Psychiatry

Western Journal of Nursing Research

Labour Studies

Canadian Labour & Employment Law Journal/Revue canadienne de droit du travail et de l'emploi

Labour, Capital and Society/Travail, capital et société

Labour/Travail: Journal of Canadian Labour Studies/Revue d'études ouvrières canadiennes

Relations industrielles/Industrial Relations

Language and Linguistics

Applied Semiotics/Sémiotique appliquée

Canadian Journal of Applied Linguistics/Revue canadienne de linguistique appliquée

Canadian Journal of Linguistics/Revue canadienne de linguistique

Canadian Modern Language Review/Revue canadienne des langues vivantes

Éducation et francophonie

Onomastica Canadiana: Journal of the Canadian Society for the Study of Names

Law

Advocates' Quarterly

Alberta Law Review

Appeal: Review of Current Law and Law Reform

Banking & Finance Law Review/Revue de droit bancaire et de finance

Cahiers de droit

Canadian Bar Review/Revue du barreau canadien

Canadian Business Law Journal/Revue canadienne du droit de commerce

Canadian Criminal Law Review/Revue canadienne de droit pénal

Canadian Family Law Quarterly/Cahier trimestriel de droit de la famille

Canadian Intellectual Property Review/Revue canadienne de propriété intellectuelle

Canadian Journal of Family Law/Revue canadienne de droit familial

Canadian Journal of Law and Jurisprudence

Canadian Journal of Law and Society/Revue canadienne droit et société

Canadian Journal of Law and Technology

Canadian Journal of Women and the Law/Revue femmes et droit

Criminal Law Quarterly

Dalhousie Law Journal

Health Law Journal

Health Law Review

Intellectual Property Journal/Revue de propriété intellectuelle

International Journal of Law and Psychiatry

Journal of Environmental Law and Practice

Journal of Law & Equality
Manitoba Law Journal
McGill Law Journal / Revue de droit de McGill
National Journal of Constitutional Law / Revue nationale de droit constitutionnel
Osgoode Hall Law Journal / Revue juridique d'Osgoode Hall
Ottawa Law Review / Revue de droit d'Ottawa
Queen's Law Journal
Review of Constitutional Studies / Revue d'études constitutionnelles
Revue juridique thémis
Saskatchewan Law Review
U.B.C. Law Review
University of New Brunswick Law Journal / Revue de droit de l'Université du Nouveau-Brunswick
University of Toronto Faculty of Law Review / Revue de droit de l'Université de Toronto
University of Toronto Law Journal
Windsor Review of Legal and Social Issues / Revue des affaires juridiques et sociales

Library and Information Studies
Argus: revue québécoise des professionnels de l'information documentaire
Canadian Journal of Information and Library Science / Revue canadienne des sciences de l'information et de bibliothéconomie
Documentation et bibliothèques
Journal of the Canadian Health Libraries Association / Journal de l'Association des bibliothèques de la santé du Canada
School Libraries in Canada
Simile: Studies in Media & Information Literacy Education

Literature
ARIEL: A Review of International English Literature
Canadian Children's Literature / Littérature canadienne pour la jeunesse
Canadian Literature / Littérature canadienne
Canadian Poetry: Studies, Documents, Reviews
Eighteenth-Century Fiction
English Studies in Canada
Essays on Canadian Writing
Études françaises
Études littéraires: théories, analyses et débats
Germano-Slavica: A Canadian Journal of Germanic and Slavic Comparative and Interdisciplinary Studies
International Fiction Review

Journal of Pre-Raphaelite Studies
Mosaic: A Journal for the Interdisciplinary Study of Literature
Renaissance and Reformation / Renaissance et réforme
Studies in Canadian Literature / Études en littérature canadienne
Texte: revue de critique et de théorie littéraire
Textual Studies in Canada / Études textuelles au Canada
Thalia: Studies in Literary Humor
Victorian Review
Voix et images: littérature québécoise

Mathematics and Statistics
Annales des sciences mathématiques du Québec
Canadian Journal of Mathematics / Journal canadien de mathématiques
Canadian Journal of Statistics / Revue canadienne de statistique
Canadian Mathematical Bulletin / Bulletin canadien de mathématiques
Dynamics of Continuous, Discrete and Impulsive Systems Series A:
   Mathematical Analysis
Dynamics of Continuous, Discrete and Impulsive Systems Series B: Applications
   and Algorithms
Theory and Applications of Categories
Utilitas Mathematica: An International Journal of Discrete and Combinatorial
   Mathematics and Statistical Design

Medicine
Canadian Association of Radiologists Journal / Journal de l'Association
   canadienne des radiologistes
Canadian Bulletin of Medical History / Bulletin canadien d'histoire de la
   médecine
Canadian Family Physician / Médecin de famille canadien
Canadian Journal of Anaesthesia / Journal canadien d'anesthésie
Canadian Journal of Cardiology / Journal canadien de cardiologie
Canadian Journal of Diagnosis
Canadian Journal of Gastroenterology / Journal canadien de gastroentérologie
Canadian Journal of Infectious Diseases & Medical Microbiology / Journal
   canadien des maladies infectieuses et de la microbiologie médicale
Canadian Journal of Neurological Sciences / Journal canadien des sciences
   neurologiques
Canadian Journal of Ophthalmology / Journal canadien d'ophtalmologie
Canadian Journal of Plastic Surgery / Journal canadien de chirurgie plastique
Canadian Journal of Psychiatry / Revue canadienne de psychiatrie
Canadian Journal of Rural Medicine / Journal canadien de la médecine rurale
Canadian Journal of Surgery / Journal canadien de chirurgie

Canadian Respiratory Journal
CJEM/JCMU: Canadian Journal of Emergency Medicine/Journal canadien de la médecine d'urgence
Clinical and Investigative Medicine/Médecine clinique et expérimentale
CMAJ/JAMC: Canadian Medical Association Journal/Journal de l'Association médicale canadienne
JOGC: Journal of Obstetrics and Gynecology Canada/Journal d'obstétrique et gynécologie du Canada
Journal of Cutaneous Medicine and Surgery
Journal of Psychiatry and Neuroscience/Revue de psychiatrie et de neuroscience
Journal of Rheumatology
Journal of Sexual & Reproductive Medicine/Journal des maladies de la fonction sexuelle et de la reproduction
Paediatrics & Child Health
Pain Research & Management
Peritoneal Dialysis International

Music

Cahiers de la Société québécoise de recherche en musique
Canadian Folk Music Bulletin/Bulletin de musique folklorique canadienne
Canadian Music Educator
Canadian University Music Review/Revue de musique des universités canadiennes
Circuit: musiques contemporaines

Native Studies

Canadian Journal of Native Education
Canadian Journal of Native Studies/Revue canadienne des études autochtones
Études/Inuit/Studies
Indigenous Law Journal
Journal of Aboriginal Economic Development
Native Studies Review

Nursing

Axon/Axone
Canadian Journal of Cardiovascular Nursing/Revue canadienne de nursing cardiovasculaire
Canadian Journal of Nursing Leadership
Canadian Journal of Nursing Research/Revue canadienne de recherche en sciences infirmières
Canadian Nurse/Infirmière canadienne
Canadian Oncology Nursing Journal/Revue canadienne de soins infirmiers en oncologie

*CANNT Journal / Journal ACITN: Canadian Association of Nephrology
Nurses and Technologists*
Dynamics: Official Journal of the Canadian Association of Critical Care Nurses
International Journal of Nursing Education Scholarship
OOHNA Journal: Ontario Occupational Health Nurses Association

Pharmacology
*Canadian Journal of Clinical Pharmacology / Journal canadien de
pharmacologie clinique*
*CJHP / JCPH: Canadian Journal of Hospital Pharmacy / Journal canadien de
la pharmacie hospitalière*
*CPJ / RPC: Canadian Pharmaceutical Journal / Revue pharmaceutique
canadienne*
JPPS: Journal of Pharmacy & Pharmaceutical Sciences

Philosophy
AE: Canadian Aesthetics Journal / Revue canadienne d'esthétique
Canadian Journal of Philosophy
Dialogue: Canadian Philosophical Review / Revue canadienne de philosophie
*Eidos: Canadian Graduate Journal of Philosophy / Revue canadienne d'études
supérieures en philosophie*
Informal Logic
Laval théologique et philosophique
Philosophia Mathematica
*Symposium: Canadian Journal of Continental Philosophy / Revue canadienne
de philosophie continentale*
*Ultimate Reality and Meaning: Interdisciplinary Studies in the Philosophy of
Understanding*

Physics
Canadian Acoustics / Acoustique canadienne
Canadian Journal of Physics / Revue canadienne de physique
Physics in Canada / Physique au Canada

Political Science
Canadian Foreign Policy / Politique étrangère du Canada
Canadian Journal of Political Science / Revue canadienne de science politique
Canadian Military Journal / Revue militaire canadienne
Études internationales
International Journal
*Isuma: Canadian Journal of Policy Research / Revue canadienne de recherche
sur les politiques*

Journal of Conflict Studies
Pacific Affairs: An International Journal of Asia and the Pacific
Peace Research: Canadian Journal of Peace Studies
Politique et sociétés

Population Studies
  Cahiers québécois de démographie
  Canadian Journal of International Migration and Integration/Revue de l'integration et de la migration internationale
  Canadian Studies in Population
  Refuge: Canada's Periodical on Refugees

Psychology
  Canadian Journal of Behavioural Science/Revue canadienne des sciences du comportement
  Canadian Journal of Career Development/Revue canadienne de développement de carrière
  Canadian Journal of Community Mental Health/Revue canadienne de santé mentale communautaire
  Canadian Journal of Counselling/Revue canadienne de counseling
  Canadian Journal of Experimental Psychology/Revue canadienne de psychologie expérimentale
  Canadian Journal of Human Sexuality
  Canadian Journal of Psychoanalysis/Revue canadienne de psychanalyse
  Canadian Psychology/Psychologie canadienne
  Canadian Undergraduate Journal of Cognitive Science
  Revue de psychoéducation et d'orientation

Public Administration
  Canadian Journal of Program Evaluation/Revue canadienne d'évaluation de programme
  Canadian Public Administration/Administration publique du Canada
  Optimum Online: Journal of Public Sector Management

Recreation and Leisure Studies
  Avante
  Canadian Journal of Applied Physiology/Revue canadienne de physiologie appliquée
  Leisure/Loisir
  Loisir et société/Society and Leisure
  Physical & Health Education Journal/Journal de l'éducation physique et l'éducation à la santé
  Sport History Review/Revue de l'histoire des sports

Religious Studies
Axis Mundi: A Student Journal for the Academic Study of Religion
Journal of Baha'i Studies / Revue des études baha'ies
Journal of Hebrew Scriptures
Journal of Mennonite Studies
Journal of Religion and Popular Culture
Journal of the Canadian Church Historical Society
McMaster Journal of Theology and Ministry
Religiologiques
Studies in Religion / Sciences religieuses
Théologiques
Toronto Journal of Theology

Social Work
Canadian Social Work
Canadian Social Work Review / Revue canadienne de service social
Currents: New Scholarship in the Human Services
Relational Child & Youth Care Practice

Sociology
Alternate Routes: A Journal of Critical Social Research
Canadian Journal of Sociology / Cahiers canadiens de sociologie
Canadian Review of Sociology and Anthropology / Revue canadienne de sociologie et d'anthropologie
Histoire sociale / Social History
Journal of Comparative Family Studies
Recherches sociographiques
Sociologie et sociétés

Theatre
Annuaire théâtral: revue québécoise d'études théâtrales
Canadian Theatre Review
Early Theatre: A Journal Associated with the Records of Early English Drama
Essays in Theatre / Études théâtrales
Modern Drama
Theatre Research in Canada / Recherches théâtrales au Canada

Veterinary Medicine
Canadian Journal of Veterinary Research / Revue canadienne de recherche vétérinaire
Canadian Veterinary Journal / Revue vétérinaire canadienne

Women's Studies
  Atlantis: A Women's Studies Journal / Revue d'études sur les femmes
  Canadian Woman Studies / Cahiers de la femme
  *RFR / DRF: Resources for Feminist Research / Documentation sur la recherche
      féministe*
  Thirdspace: Journal for Emerging Feminist Scholars
  Women in Judaism: A Multidisciplinary Journal
  *Women's Health and Urban Life: An International and Interdisciplinary
      Journal*

Appendix B

A List of 20 Dictionaries, 6 Thesauruses, and 18 Style Manuals

Dictionaries

General Dictionaries

Barber, K. (Ed.). (2001). *The Canadian Oxford dictionary*. Don Mills, ON: Oxford University Press.

de Wolf, G. D., et al. (Eds.). (2000). *Gage Canadian dictionary* (Rev. and expanded). Vancouver, BC: Gage Educational Publishing.

Green, S., et al. (Eds.). (1998). *ITP Nelson Canadian dictionary of the English language: An encyclopedic reference*. Toronto, ON: ITP Nelson.

Mish, F. C., et al. (Eds.). (2003). *Merriam-Webster's collegiate dictionary* (11th ed.). Springfield, MA: Merriam-Webster.

Pickett, J. P., et al. (Eds.). (2000). *The American heritage dictionary of the English language* (4th ed.). Boston, MA: Houghton Mifflin.

Subject-related Dictionaries

Allaby, M. (Ed.). (1999). *A dictionary of zoology* (2nd ed.). New York: Oxford University Press.

Anderson, D. M., Keith, J., Novak, P. D., & Elliot, M. A. (2002). *Mosby's medical, nursing, and allied health dictionary* (6th ed.). St. Louis, MO: Mosby.

Borowski, E. J., & Borwein, J. M. (Eds.). (2002). *Collins dictionary of mathematics* (2nd ed.). Glasgow: HarperCollins.

Dobroslavic, T. (Comp.). (1994). *The Canadian dictionary of abbreviations* (2nd ed., Rev.). Toronto, ON: ECW Press.

Dukelow, D. A., & Nuse, B. (1995). *The dictionary of Canadian law* (2nd ed.). Scarborough, ON: Carswell.

Edgar, K. J. (Ed.). (2004). *Acronyms, initialisms and abbreviations dictionary* (33rd ed., Vols. 1–4). Farmington Hills, MI: Gale.

Isaacs, A. (Ed.). (2000). *A dictionary of physics* (4th ed.). New York: Oxford University Press.

McGraw-Hill dictionary of scientific and technical terms (6th ed.). (2003). New York: McGraw-Hill.

Merriam-Webster's geographical dictionary (3rd ed.). (1997). Springfield, MA: Merriam-Webster.

Mitton, J. (2001). *Cambridge dictionary of astronomy.* New York: Cambridge University Press.

Pfaffenberger, B. (Comp.). (2000). *Webster's new world dictionary of computer terms* (8th ed.). Foster City, CA: IDG Books Worldwide.

Rutherford, D. (2002). *Routledge dictionary of economics* (2nd ed.). New York: Routledge.

Singleton, P., & Sainsbury, D. (2002). *Dictionary of microbiology and molecular biology* (3rd ed.). New York: Wiley.

Troeh, F. R., & Donohue, R. L. (2000). *Dictionary of agriculture and environmental science.* Ames, IA: Iowa State Press.

Upton, G., & Cook, I. (Eds.). (2002). *A dictionary of statistics.* New York: Oxford University Press.

Thesauruses

Chambers, J. K., & Munro, C. (2001). *Fitzhenry & Whiteside Canadian thesaurus.* Markham, ON: Fitzhenry & Whiteside.

Kipfer, B. A., & Chapman, R. L. (Eds.). (2001). *Roget's international thesaurus* (6th ed.). New York: HarperResource.

Laird, C. (Ed.). (2000). *Webster's new world thesaurus* (4th ed.). New York: Wiley.

Pontisso, R. (Ed.). (2004). *Paperback Oxford Canadian thesaurus.* Don Mills, ON: Oxford University Press.

Pratt, T. K., et al. (Eds.). (1998). *Gage Canadian thesaurus.* Vancouver, BC: Gage Educational Publishing.

Stein, J., & Flexner, S. B. (Eds.). (2000). *Random House Roget's college thesaurus* (Rev. and updated by E. Pearsons & C. G. Braham). New York: Random House.

Style Manuals

American Institute of Physics. (1990). *AIP style manual* (4th ed.). New York: Author.

American Management Association. (1996). *The AMA style guide for business writing.* New York: AMACOM.

American Mathematical Society. (1996). *The AMS author handbook: General instructions for preparing manuscripts* (Rev. ed.). Providence, RI: Author.

American Psychological Association. (2001). *Publication manual of the American Psychological Association* (5th ed.). Washington, DC: Author.

American Society for Microbiology. (1991). *ASM style manual for journals and books.* Washington, DC: Author.

Bates, R. L., Adkins-Heljeson, M. D., & Buchanan, R. C. (Eds.). (1995).

Geowriting: A guide to writing, editing and printing in earth science (5th ed.). Alexandria, VA: American Geological Institute.

Council of Biology Editors, Style Manual Committee. (1994). *Scientific style and format: The CBE manual for authors, editors, and publishers* (6th ed.). New York: Cambridge University Press.

Dodd, J. S. (Ed.). (1997). *The ACS style guide: A manual for authors and editors* (2nd ed.). Washington, DC: American Chemical Society.

Gibaldi, J. (1998). *MLA style manual and guide to scholarly publishing* (2nd ed.). New York: The Modern Language Association of America.

Gibaldi, J. (2003). *MLA handbook for writers of research papers* (6th ed.). New York: The Modern Language Association of America.

Higham, N. J. (1998). *A handbook of writing for the mathematical sciences* (2nd ed.). Philadelphia, PA: Society for Industrial and Applied Mathematics.

International Committee of Medical Journal Editors. (1997, January 15). Uniform requirements for manuscripts submitted to biomedical journals. *CMAJ: Canadian Medical Association Journal, 156*(2), 270–277. Updates available at http://www.icmje.org

Iverson, C., Flanagin, A., Fontanarosa, P. B., Glass, R. M., Glitman, P., Lantz, J. C., et al. (1998). *American Medical Association manual of style: A guide for authors and editors* (9th ed.). Baltimore, MD: Williams & Wilkins.

McGill Law Journal. (2002). *Canadian guide to uniform legal citation* (5th ed.). Scarborough, ON: Carswell.

Thibault, D. (1990). *Bibliographic style manual.* Ottawa, ON: National Library of Canada.

Turabian, K. L. (1996). *A manual for writers of term papers, theses, and dissertations* (6th ed., Rev. by J. Grossman & A. Bennett). Chicago, IL: University of Chicago Press.

University of Chicago Press. (2003). *The Chicago manual of style* (15th ed.). Chicago, IL: Author.

Walker, J. R., & Taylor, T. W. (1998). *The Columbia guide to online style.* New York: Columbia University Press.

Appendix C

A List of 150 Informal and Formal Expressions

Informal	*Formal*
ad	advertisement
a lot	much
anyways	anyway
anywheres	anywhere
artsy	pretentiously artistic
awfully	rather
booze	alcoholic drink
buck	dollar
buddy	friend
budgie	parakeet
burg	city or town
bushed	exhausted
bust	arrest or break
chicken	coward
cinch	easy
clobber	batter
clueless	ignorant
combo	small band
condo	condominium
cool it	calm down or relax
cop	police officer
crackerjack	expert
dander	temper
debunk	disprove

detox	detoxification
divvy	divide
enthuse	show enthusiasm
exam	examination
expecting	pregnant
fellow	boy or man
finagle	act dishonestly
flu	influenza
flunk	fail
forty winks	short sleep
frat	fraternity
frazzle	wear out
freebie	no charge
freeloader	parasite
fridge	refrigerator
gig	musical engagement
glitzy	gaudy
gooey	sticky
goon	thug
gouge	overcharge
gripe	complain
grub	food
guck	sludge
gutsy	courageous
guy	man
gyp	cheat
hacker	computer enthusiast
hang in	persist

hang-up	fixation
hanky-panky	dishonest behaviour
hassle	annoy
hatchet job	fierce attack
haywire	erratic
heist	robbery
hock	pawn
hooker	prostitute
hooky (play)	truant (play)
hoopla	commotion
horse sense	common sense
hot air	empty talk
hype	intense promotion
iffy	uncertain
ism	doctrine or theory
jinx	unlucky
jitters	extreme nervousness
kickback	secret payment
kid	child or tease
kind of	rather
lab	laboratory
laid-back	easygoing
leery	wary
lemon	defective product
lots (of)	much
lousy	bad or mean
memo	memorandum
mike	microphone

moonlight	work at a second job
mug	face or mouth
nab	arrest
nifty	clever
nitty-gritty	harsh truth
nosh	snack
nosy	prying
okay (OK)	all right
once-over	quick inspection
one-liner	witty remark
one-upmanship	competitive advantage
phony	fake
photo	photograph
picky	fussy
pitch in	help
put-down	snub
quote	quotation
rag	newspaper
raring	eager
razzle-dazzle	pageantry
rehab	rehabilitation
rip-off	exploit
rock	diamond
rookie	novice
sashay	strut
savvy	understanding
scam	fraudulent scheme
scope	microscope or telescope

scrounge	beg
shades	sunglasses
show biz	show business
sidekick	companion
slammer	jail
sleuth	detective
slip-up	blunder
small time	unimportant
snitch	steal
snoop	pry
snooze	nap
softie	sentimental person
sort of	rather
spiel	harangue
spiffy	stylish
splurge	spend lavishly
spooky	eerie
stuck-up	conceited
stunning	strikingly attractive
surefire	certain
tacky	tasteless
tick	credit
tightwad	miser
tony	high-class
trendy	fashionable
typo	typographical error
umpteen	great many
up-and-coming	promising

uptight	tense
veggies	vegetables
vibes	feelings
wacky	eccentric
way-out	unconventional
weirdo	strange person
windbag	bore
wisecrack	flippant remark
Xmas	Christmas
yank	sudden pull
yen	yearning
yummy	delicious
zilch	nothing
zillion	indefinite large number

Note. Informal expressions are sometimes used in formal writing when there is no formal counterpart. Place quotation marks around informal words used in formal writing (e.g., "techie"). They tell the reader that you deliberately chose the word to convey a nuance that a formal word cannot convey.

Appendix D

A List of 100 Tautologies

(advance) reservations

(advance) warning

(all) throughout

(already) under way

and (moreover)

as a (general) rule

(bad) nightmare

(basic) essentials

blue (in colour)

(brief) synopsis

(broad) generalization

(carefully) examine

(clearly) evident

climb (up)

(close) proximity

(complete) consensus

(complete) gamut

(complete) monopoly

(completely) immersed

(completely) unanimous

component (parts)

(concise) summary

consensus (of opinion)

cooperate (together)

(cultural) tradition

(dead) standstill

(deliberate) lie

depreciate (in value)

descend (down)

(different) varieties

(direct) quotation

(early) beginnings

elective (course)

eliminate (completely)

(empty) void

(equal) halves

(evil) curse

(fellow) colleagues

few (in number)

filled (to capacity)

(first) began

(foreign) import

(formal) requisition

(free) gift

(future) prospects

(gifted) genius

grouped (together)

(hard) struggle

(harmonious) peace

(honest) truth

(hot) boiling water

(inner) core

isolated (and alone)

join (together)

large (in size)

(major) breakthrough

mix (together)

(mutual) cooperation

(mutually) agreeable

(necessary) requisite

(new) innovation

(old) adage

one (single)

(over) exaggerate

(passing) fad

(past) experience

period (of time)

(positive) benefits

proceed (ahead)

(really) unique

(redundant) rehash

repeat (again)

return (back)

(rich) millionaire

(round) circles

rules (and regulations)

(rural) countryside

(sad) mourners

(separate) entities

(serious) emergency

(single) unit

(small) pittance

smile (on his face)

stunted (in growth)

(sudden) surprise

sufficient (enough)

(sum) total

(tall) skyscrapers

(temporary) loan

throughout (the entire)

(total) blank

(twelve) noon

(ultimate) end

undergraduate (student)

(unsubstantiated) rumour

(vertical) column

visible (to the eye)

winter (season)

worthy (of merit)

(young) infant

Appendix E

A List of 120 Circumlocutions With Abridgements

Circumlocution	*Abridgement*
a great deal of	much
a large number of	many
a majority of	most
a small (limited) number of	few/several
a sufficient number of	enough
ahead of schedule	early
all by myself	alone
along the lines of	like/similar to
are of the same opinion	agree
as a matter of fact	in fact
as can be seen	obviously
as has already been indicated	as stated
as of this date	today
as soon as possible	promptly
at a later date	later
at an earlier date	earlier
at the moment	now
at the present time	now
at this point in time	now
backed by a reference	documented
based on the fact that	because
be in possession of	to have
bring to a conclusion	conclude/end/finish
by the same token	similarly

despite the fact that	although
due to the fact that	because
during the course of	during
during the month of January	in January
each and every one of you	all
far from sure	unsure
first of all	first
for the purpose of	for
for the simple reason that	because/since
from that point on	henceforth
from the standpoint of	according to
give rise to	cause
goes under the name of	is called
had the occasion to be	was
has a tendency to	tends to
has the ability to	can
have been shown to be	are
have need for	need
in a position to	can
in a satisfactory manner	satisfactorily
in a similar manner	likewise
in advance of	before
in all cases	always
incapable of functioning	dysfunctional
in close proximity to	near
in light of the fact that	because
in many cases	often
in most cases	usually

in order to	to
in possession of	has
in spite of the fact that	although
in the classroom situation	in class
in the direction of	toward
in the event that	if
in the final analysis	finally
in the last little while	recently
in the not too distant future	soon
in the process (course) of	during
in the same way	like
in view of the fact that	because
it can be seen that	therefore/thus
it goes without saying	clearly
it has been shown in the literature	evidence shows
it is apparent therefore that	hence/thus
it is evident that	clearly
it is no secret that	clearly
it is often the case that	often
it is the intention of this writer to	I will
it is this author's opinion	I believe
it must be remembered that	remember
it would appear that	apparently
lacks the ability to	cannot
make reference to	refer to
make up your mind	decide
more often than not	usually
not in a position to	cannot

of considerable magnitude	large
on a daily basis	daily
on a regular basis	regularly
on a theoretical level	in theory
on account of	because
on the grounds that	because
on the verge of	about to
on two separate occasions	twice
outside of the country	abroad
owing to the fact that	because
put in an appearance	appear
regardless of the fact that	although
render assistance to	help
somewhere in the vicinity of	near
stay away from	avoid
the great majority	most
the question as to whether	whether
the work that they were doing	their work
there is no doubt	undoubtedly
throughout the world	worldwide
time and time again	repeatedly
to arrive at a decision	to decide
to be able to	can
to be in agreement	to agree
to be of the opinion that	to believe
to begin with	first
to make an adjustment to	to adjust
to make use of	to use

to point out the fact that	to illustrate
to quote directly from a source	to cite
to take into consideration	to consider
until such time as	until
up to this point in time	to date
was witness to	witnessed
we wish to thank you	we thank you
which goes by the name of	called
will take on the format of	will look like
with regard to	about/concerning
with the exception of	except for
without any charge	free

Appendix F

A List of 50 Euphemisms With Translations

Euphemism	*Translation*
adult entertainment	pornography
air support	bombing
beauty spot	freckle or mole
blemish	pimple
body moisture	sweat
chemical dependency	drug addiction
collateral damage	civilian casualties
conflict	war
digital imaging	fingerprinting
disengage	retreat
disinformation	lie
disposal area	dump
economically deprived	poor
encore telecast	television rerun
ethnic cleansing	genocide
exotic dancer	stripper
expectorate	spit
fabrication	lie
funeral director	undertaker
incident	accident or crisis
inebriated	drunk
inoperative statement	lie
interment	burial
job action	strike or work-to-rule

memorial gardens	cemetery
neutralize	kill
passed away	died
plus size	large
preowned	used
price adjustment	price increase
private parts	the genitals
problem skin	acne
public assistance	welfare
reconditioned	secondhand
regurgitate	vomit
revenue enhancement	tax increase
sales associate	store clerk
security breach	break-in
senior citizen	older person
service interruption	power failure
social disease	venereal disease
social unrest	demonstrations or riots
spent fuel	radioactive waste
street people	the homeless
subsidy publisher	vanity press
terminate	dismiss or fire
underarm wetness	sweat
underprivileged	poor
vertically challenged	short
waste material	garbage

Appendix G

A List of 100 Clichés

a cut above

a loose cannon

a time bomb

a wake up call

add insult to injury

after all is said and done

all walks of life

almighty dollar

as luck would have it

as plain as day

back to square one

beginning of the end

believe it or not

better late than never

bite the bullet

boggles the mind

bone of contention

bread and butter issue

budding genius

by hook or by crook

calm before the storm

cut to the chase

down the road

dull as dust

few and far between

first and foremost

food for thought

for better or for worse

for what it is worth

foregone conclusion

gentle as a lamb

giant step forward

grind to a halt

hard and fast

harsh reality

hook, line, and sinker

in a nutshell

in the final analysis

in the nick of time

in this day and age

kiss of death

labour of love

last but not least

light as a feather

lock, stock, and barrel

meaningful dialogue

method in their madness

mind over matter

mixed blessing

name of the game

needless to say

no guts, no glory

no easy answer

no sooner said than done

no stone unturned

of the first magnitude

on the ball

only time will tell

paid the price

part and parcel

pen to paper

picture of health

place in the sun

playing with fire

practise what you preach

publish or perish

reinvent the wheel

remains to be seen

road to recovery

rude awakening

school of hard knocks

second to none

short and sweet

sigh of relief

slow and steady

slowly but surely

smooth as silk

sober as a judge

solid as a rock

spirited debate

stands to reason

stiff upper lip

straight and narrow

the bottom line

the cutting edge

the simple truth

the thing to do

thick as thieves

through thick and thin

time honoured

to a tee

to the bitter end

tried and true

true to form

under the weather

up in arms

winds of change

word to the wise

wrapped in mystery

writing on the wall

Appendix H

A List of 24 Directories and Guides

Database Directory

Mueckenheim, J. K. (Ed.). (2004). *Gale directory of databases* (Vols. 1–2, Pt. 2). Farmington Hills, MI: Gale. (Rev. and updated semiannually)

Periodical Directories

Hedblad, A. (Ed.). (2004). *Gale directory of publications and broadcast media* (138th ed., Vols. 1–5). Farmington Hills, MI: Gale. (Annual)

Or *Gale directory of publications and broadcast media.* [On-line] http://www.galenet.com

Or *Gale directory of publications and broadcast media.* [CD-ROM] Farmington Hills, MI: Gale.

MLA directory of periodicals. [On-line] (2005). New York: The Modern Language Association of America. http://www.mla.org (Updated semiannually)

Or *MLA directory of periodicals.* [CD-ROM] New York: The Modern Language Association of America.

Mogge, D. W., & Budka, P. (Eds.). (2000). *Directory of scholarly electronic journals and academic discussion lists.* Washington, DC: Association of Research Libraries.

Or *Directory of scholarly electronic journals and academic discussion lists.* [On-line] http://www.arl.org/scomm/edir/archive.html

Striplin, D. (Ed.). (2004). *Standard periodical directory* (27th ed.). New York: Oxbridge. (Annual)

Or *Standard periodical directory.* [On-line] http://www.
mediafinder.com

Or *Standard periodical directory.* [CD-ROM] New York: Oxbridge.

Ulrich's periodicals directory (44th ed., Vols. 1–4). (2005). New
Providence, NJ: R.R. Bowker. (Annual)

Or *Ulrich's periodicals directory.* [On-line] http://www.ulrichsweb.
com

Or *Ulrich's on disc.* [CD-ROM] New Providence, NJ: R. R.
Bowker.

Publisher Directories

Behrens, M., et al. (Eds.). (2004). *The book trade in Canada* (2005 ed.).
Toronto, ON: Quill & Quire. (Annual)

Books in print 2005-2006 (Vols. 1–8). (2005). New Providence, NJ: R.
R. Bowker. (Annual)

Or *Books in print.com professional* [On-line] http://www.
booksinprint.com/bip/

Or *Books in print on disc.* [CD-ROM] New Providence, NJ: R. R.
Bowker.

Or *Books in print on disc - Canadian edition.* [CD-ROM] New
Providence, NJ: R. R. Bowker.

Or *Books in print with book reviews on disc.* [CD-ROM] New
Providence, NJ: R. R. Bowker.

Or *Books in print with book reviews on disc - Canadian edition.* [CD-
ROM] New Providence, NJ: R. R. Bowker.

Or *Global books in print.com* [On-line] http://www.
globalbooksinprint.com/GlobalBooksInPrint

Or *Global books in print on disc.* [CD-ROM] New Providence, NJ:
R. R. Bowker.

Brogan, K. (Ed.). (2004). *Guide to literary agents 2005.* Cincinnati, OH:

F+W Publications. (Annual)

Brogan, K. S., & Brewer, R. (Eds.). (2003). *Writer's market 2004*. Cincinnati, OH: F+W Publications. (Annual)

Or *Writer's market 2004 online*. http://www.WritersMarket.com

Butler, M. (Ed.). (2004). *Canadian books in print: Author and title index*. Toronto, ON: University of Toronto Press. (Annual)

Butler, M. (Ed.). (2004). *Canadian books in print: Subject index*. Toronto, ON: University of Toronto Press. (Annual)

Gagné, L. (Ed.). (2005). *Publishers directory* (28th ed.). Farmington Hills, MI: Gale. (Annual)

Hallard, K., et al. (Eds.). (2003). *International literary market place 2004*. Medford, NJ: Information Today. (Annual)

Or *International literary market place*. [On-line] http://www.literarymarketplace.com

Hallard, K., et al. (Eds.). (2003). *Literary market place 2004* (Vols. 1–2). Medford, NJ: Information Today. (Annual)

Or *Literary market place*. [On-line] http://www.literarymarketplace.com

Herman, J. (2003). *Jeff Herman's guide to book publishers, editors, & literary agents* (2004 ed.). New York: Watson-Guptill Publications. (Annual)

Subject guide to books in print 2005-2006 (Vols. 1–6). (2005). New Providence, NJ: R. R. Bowker. (Annual)

Tooze, S. B. (2004). *The Canadian writer's market* (16th Rev. ed.). Toronto, ON: McClelland & Stewart. (Annual)

Turner, B. (Ed.). (2003). *The writer's handbook 2004*. London: Macmillan.

Whitaker's books in print (Vols. 1–5). (2003). London: Whitaker. (Annual)

Indexing Guides

Bonura, L. S. (1994). *The art of indexing*. New York: Wiley.

Lancaster, F. W. (2003). *Indexing and abstracting in theory and practice* (3rd ed.). Champaign, IL: University of Illinois, Graduate School of Library and Information Science.

Mulvany, N. C. (2005). *Indexing books* (2nd ed.). Chicago, IL: University of Chicago Press.

Wellisch, H. H. (1996). *Indexing from A to Z* (2nd ed., Rev. and enlarged). New York: H. W. Wilson.

Appendix I

A List of 50 Canadian and American Spellings

Canadian	American
abridgement	abridgment
acknowledgement	acknowledgment
agendas	agenda
anaesthetic	anesthetic
appendices	appendixes
axe	ax
behaviour	behavior
bursae	bursas
cancelled	canceled
catalogue	catalog
centre	center
châteaux	chateaus
cheque (bank draft)	check
colloquia	colloquiums
counsellor	counselor
defence	defense
discolour	discolor
favourite	favorite
fibre	fiber
flyer	flier
grey	gray
honourable	honorable
jewellery	jewelry
kilometre	kilometer

labelled	labeled
licence (noun)	license (noun)
likeable	likable
litre	liter
manoeuvre	maneuver
memoranda	memorandums
mould	mold
moustache	mustache
neighbour	neighbor
offence	offense
omelette	omelet
orthopaedics	orthopedics
practise (verb)	practice (verb)
pyjamas	pajamas
racquet	racket
referendums	referenda
saleable	salable
skilful	skillful
smoulder	smolder
storey (floor)	story
sulphur	sulfur
syllabuses	syllabi
theatre	theater
tranquility	tranquillity
whisky	whiskey
woollen	woolen

Appendix J

A List of 100 Commonly Misspelled Words

Misspelling	*Correct Spelling*
accessable	accessible
accomodate	accommodate
acheivement	achievement
acquited	acquitted
acumulate	accumulate
administrater	administrator
adviseable	advisable
affadevit	affidavit
alotted	allotted
alright	all right
alysum	alyssum
annoint	anoint
architectual	architectural
baccaleaurate	baccalaureate
bankrupcy	bankruptcy
barbituate	barbiturate
batalion	battalion
calender	calendar
carburator	carburetor
changable	changeable
colonnel	colonel
committment	commitment
compliant **for**	complaint
concensus	consensus

concience	conscience
concuring	concurring
connoiseur	connoisseur
consistant	consistent
dairy **for**	diary
desert **for**	dessert
desparate	desperate
diaphram	diaphragm
disray	disarray
drunkeness	drunkenness
embarass	embarrass
erronous	erroneous
exerpt	excerpt
existance	existence
familar	familiar
feasability	feasibility
garantee	guarantee
goverment	government
grammer	grammar
guage	gauge
harrass	harass
hemorage	hemorrhage
heresay	hearsay
hinderance	hindrance
hinderland	hinterland
homogenous	homogeneous
inate	innate
indispensible	indispensable

initative	initiative
innoculate	inoculate
irrate	irate
irresistable	irresistible
irrevelant	irrelevant
judical	judicial
labratory	laboratory
liasion	liaison
mispelled	misspelled
moral **for**	morale
nieve	naive
nineth	ninth
opthamology	ophthalmology
perogative	prerogative
plagarism	plagiarism
preceed	precede
priviledge	privilege
procede	proceed
questionaire	questionnaire
rational **for**	rationale
receipe	recipe
referred **for**	refereed
resevoir	reservoir
rythm	rhythm
sacreligious	sacrilegious
seperate	separate
shedule	schedule
similiar	similar

sophmore	sophomore
speciment	specimen
suble	subtle
supercede	supersede
temperment	temperament
themselfs	themselves
through **for**	thorough
tradgedy	tragedy
trail **for**	trial
twelveth	twelfth
undoubedly	undoubtedly
useage	usage
vaccum	vacuum
vengance	vengeance
villify	vilify
waring	warring
whereever	wherever
wierd	weird
wintery	wintry
withold	withhold

Appendix K

A List of 50 Homonyms

advice (noun – opinion – That was sound advice.)
advise (verb – to counsel – We advise you to stay home.)

affect (verb – to influence)
effect (noun – the result; verb – to bring about)

aisle (noun – passageway)
isle (noun – small island)

all ready (adjective phrase – They are all ready to go.)
already (adverb – Have they finished already?)

all together (adjective phrase – They are all together.)
altogether (adverb – Altogether [in total] 50 teachers were
    there.)

all ways (adjective + noun – every direction)
always (adverb – on every occasion)

allusion (noun – indirect mention)
illusion (noun – an erroneous perception)

altar (noun – The altar was at the front of the church.)
alter (verb – to change)

ascent (noun – an upward slope)
assent (noun – an agreement; verb – to agree)

borough (noun – a self-governing, incorporated town)
burro (noun – a small donkey)

burrow (noun – a hole dug in the ground by a small animal; verb – to dig)

callous (adjective – insensitive)

callus (noun – hardened tissue)

canvas (noun – cloth)

canvass (verb – to poll, to solicit)

carat (noun – a unit of weight; also spelled karat)

caret (noun – a proofreader's symbol)

carrot (noun – a vegetable)

censer (noun – an incense vessel)

censor (noun – an official who examines literature; verb – to screen)

sensor (noun – a device that responds to a stimulus)

cite (verb – to quote an authority)

sight (noun – the faculty of vision)

site (noun – the place where something is located)

complement (noun – that which completes)

compliment (noun – praise; verb – to pay a compliment)

council (noun – an assembly of individuals)

counsel (noun – advice; verb – to advise)

decent (adjective – acceptable standards of propriety)

descent (noun – downward incline or passage, lineage)

dissent (noun – disagreement; verb – to disagree)

dieing (verb – to cut or stamp with a die)

dyeing (verb – to colour material)

dying (verb – to cease living)

discreet (adjective – modest, unobtrusive)
discrete (adjective – distinct parts)

dual (adjective – double)
duel (noun – combat between two persons)

elicit (verb – to draw forth)
illicit (adjective – illegal)

emerge (verb – to come forth or rise up)
immerge (verb – to submerge)

emigrate (verb – to leave one country to settle in another)
immigrate (verb – to enter and settle in a foreign country)

eminent (adjective – outstanding, prominent)
immanent (adjective – inherent, within the mind)
imminent (adjective – about to occur)

faze (verb – to disturb)
phase (noun – stage, step, period)

foreword (noun – introductory note, preface)
forward (adjective – progressive, towards the front; noun – player)

forth (adverb – forward in time, place, or order)
fourth (noun – the ordinal number four in a series)

hoard (noun – cache, treasure; verb – to accumulate by saving or hiding)
horde (noun – swarm of people, animals, or insects)

hoarse (adjective – a harsh voice)

horse (noun – an animal)

indict (verb – to accuse of or charge with a crime)

indite (verb – to write)

ingenious (adjective – clever)

ingenuous (adjective – naive)

lean (adjective – thin; verb – to incline)

lien (noun – the right to take, hold, and sell the property of a debtor as security or payment for a debt)

loath (adjective – disinclined, reluctant)

loathe (verb – to detest)

manner (noun – behaviour, style)

manor (noun – a mansion)

mantel (noun – ornamental facing around a fireplace)

mantle (noun – loose, sleeveless coat worn over outer garments; verb – to cloak, conceal)

may be (verb – It may be wrong.)

maybe (adverb – perhaps – Maybe it is not wrong.)

naval (adjective – pertaining to the navy)

navel (noun – the umbilicus)

pair (noun – two corresponding persons or items)

pare (verb – to remove by peeling)

pear (noun – the fruit of a pear tree)

populace (noun – common people, masses)

populous (adjective – thickly populated)

pray (verb – to say a prayer)
prey (noun – a creature hunted for food)

precedence (noun – a ceremonial order, priority)
precedents (noun – conventions, previous judicial decisions)

principal (adjective – first, foremost; noun – chief, school principal)
principle (noun – general law, rule)

prophecy (noun – a prediction)
prophesy (verb – to predict)

stationary (adjective – fixed in position)
stationery (noun – writing material)

veracious (adjective – honest, precise)
voracious (adjective – greedy, ravenous)

waive (verb – to relinquish)
wave (noun – a ridge or swell moving along the surface of a body of water; verb – to move up and down)

weather (noun – atmospheric conditions)
whether (conjunction – if it is)

whine (verb – to utter a high-pitched, protracted sound)
wine (noun – an alcoholic beverage)

yoke (noun – a crossbar with a double harness; verb – to harness a draft animal)
yolk (noun – the yellow part of an egg)

References

One must be a wise reader to quote wisely and well.

A. B. Alcott

Alley, M. (1996). *The craft of scientific writing* (3rd ed.). New York: Springer-Verlag.

American Psychological Association. (2001). *Publication manual of the American Psychological Association* (5th ed.). Washington, DC: Author.

Ashton-Jones, E. (1997). Coauthoring for scholarly publication: Should you collaborate? In J. M. Moxley & T. Taylor (Eds.), *Writing and publishing for academic authors* (2nd ed., pp. 175–192). Lanham, MD: Rowman & Littlefield.

Babbie, E. (2001). *The practice of social research* (9th ed.). Toronto, ON: Wadsworth.

Barlow, R. G. (1992). Form in the preparation of scholarly manuscripts. *Scholarly Publishing, 23*(4), 243–247.

Barnet, S., Stubbs, M., Bellanca, P., & Stimpson, P. G. (2003). *The practical guide to writing: With readings and handbook* (Canadian ed.). Toronto, ON: Pearson Education Canada.

Best, J. W., & Kahn, J. V. (2006). *Research in education* (10th ed.). Toronto, ON: Allyn & Bacon.

Blicq, R., & Moretto, L. (1999). *Technically-write!* (5th ed.). Upper Saddle River, NJ: Prentice-Hall.

Boice, R. (1990). *Professors as writers: A self-help guide to productive writing.* Stillwater, OK: New Forums Press.

Boice, R. (1993). Writing blocks and tacit knowledge. *Journal of Higher Education, 64*(1), 19–54.

Brusaw, C. T., Alred, G. J., & Oliu, W. E. (1997). *Handbook of technical writing* (5th ed.). New York: St. Martin's Press.

Canadian Advisory Council on the Status of Women. (1984). *Guidelines for non-sexist writing*. Ottawa, ON: Author.

Canadian Intellectual Property Office. (2005). *A guide to copyrights*. Gatineau, QC: Industry Canada.

Cantor, J. A. (1993). *A guide to academic writing*. Westport, CT: Praeger.

CCH Canadian Ltd. v. Law Society of Upper Canada, [2004] 1 S.C.R. 339, reversing 212 D.L.R. (4th) 385 (F.C.A.), reversing in part 179 D.L.R. (4th) 609 (F.C.T.D.).

Cohen, J. (1988). *Statistical power analysis for the behavioral sciences* (2nd ed.). Hillsdale, NJ: Lawrence Erlbaum Associates.

Cragg, C., Czarnecki, B., Phillips, I. H., & Vanderlinden, K. (2000). *Editing Canadian English* (2nd ed.). Toronto, ON: Macfarlane Walter & Ross.

Day, A. (1996). *How to get research published in journals*. Brookfield, VT: Gower.

Day, R. A. (1998). *How to write and publish a scientific paper* (5th ed.). Phoenix, AZ: Oryx Press.

de Wolf, G. D., et al. (Eds.). (2000). *Gage Canadian dictionary* (Rev. and expanded). Vancouver, BC: Gage Educational Publishing.

Doyle, M. (1995). *The A-Z of non-sexist language*. London: The Women's Press.

Elbow, P. (1998). *Writing with power* (2nd ed.). New York: Oxford University Press.

Elmes, D. G., Kantowitz, B. H., & Roediger, H. L., III. (2003). *Research methods in psychology* (7th ed.). Toronto, ON: Wadsworth.

Euben, D. R. (2002). Publish or perish: The ever-higher publications hurdle for tenure. *Academe, 88*(4), 78.

Fee, M., & McAlpine, J. (1997). *Guide to Canadian English usage*. Don Mills, ON: Oxford University Press.

Fleras, A., & Elliott, J. L. (2003). *Unequal relations: An introduction to race and ethnic dynamics in Canada* (4th ed.). Toronto, ON: Pearson Education Canada.

Fox, M. F. (1994). Scientific misconduct and editorial and peer review processes. *Journal of Higher Education, 65*(3), 298–309.

Frank, F. W., & Treichler, P. A. (1989). *Language, gender, and professional writing: Theoretical approaches and guidelines for nonsexist usage.* New York: The Modern Language Association of America.

Franklin and Marshall College Writing Center and Women Aware. (1986). *(S)He: A guide to nonsexist language* (2nd ed.). Lancaster, PA: Author.

Funston, B. W., & Meehan, E. (Eds.). (1994). *Canadian constitutional documents consolidated.* Scarborough, ON: Carswell.

Gall, M. D., Gall, J. P., & Borg, W. R. (2003). *Educational research: An introduction* (7th ed.). Toronto, ON: Pearson Education.

Gastel, B. (1998). *Health writer's handbook.* Ames, IA: Iowa State University Press.

Glass, G. V., McGaw, B., & Smith, M. L. (1981). *Meta-analysis in social research.* Newbury Park, CA: Sage.

Harman, E., Montagnes, I., McMenemy, S., & Bucci, C. (Eds.). (2003). *The thesis and the book: A guide for first-time academic authors* (2nd ed.). Toronto, ON: University of Toronto Press.

Harris, L. E. (2001). *Canadian copyright law* (3rd ed.). Toronto, ON: McGraw-Hill Ryerson.

Harris, R. L. (1999). *Information graphics: A comprehensive illustrated reference.* New York: Oxford University Press.

Harsanyi, M. A. (1993). Multiple authors, multiple problems— bibliometrics and the study of scholarly collaboration: A literature review. *Library & Information Science Research, 15*(4), 325–346.

Henson, K. T. (1997). Writing for publication: Some perennial mistakes. *Phi Delta Kappan, 78*(10), 781–784.

Henson, K. T. (1999). *Writing for professional publication: Keys to academic and business success.* Needham Heights, MA: Allyn & Bacon.

Huck, S. W., & Cormier, W. H. (1996). *Reading statistics and research* (2nd ed.). New York: HarperCollins.

Human Resources Development Canada, Office for Disability Issues. (2002). *A way with words and images: Guidelines for the portrayal of persons with disabilities.* Ottawa, ON: Author.

Huth, E. J. (1990). *How to write and publish papers in the medical sciences* (2nd ed.). Baltimore, MD: Williams & Wilkins.

Huth, E. J. (1999). *Writing and publishing in medicine* (3rd ed.). Baltimore, MD: Williams & Wilkins.

Jackson, W. (1999). *Methods: Doing social research* (2nd ed.). Scarborough, ON: Prentice-Hall Canada.

King, C. R., McGuire, D. B., Longman, A. J., & Carroll-Johnson, R. M. (1997). Peer review, authorship, ethics, and conflict of interest. *Image: Journal of Nursing Scholarship, 29* (2), 163–167.

LaFollette, M. C. (1992). *Stealing into print: Fraud, plagiarism, and misconduct in scientific publishing*. Berkeley, CA: University of California Press.

Luey, B. (2002). *Handbook for academic authors* (4th ed.). New York: Cambridge University Press.

Lunsford, A., Connors, R., & Segal, J. Z. (1995). *The St. Martin's handbook for Canadians* (2nd ed.). Scarborough, ON: Nelson Canada.

Maggio, R. (1992). *The bias-free word finder: A dictionary of nondiscriminatory language*. Boston, MA: Beacon Press.

Maggio, R. (1997). *Talking about people: A guide to fair and accurate language*. Phoenix, AZ: Oryx Press.

Markel, M. (1994). *Writing in the technical fields: A step-by-step guide for engineers, scientists, and technicians*. Piscataway, NJ: IEEE Press.

McArthur, T. (Ed.). (1992). *The Oxford companion to the English language*. New York: Oxford University Press.

McMillan, A. D. (1995). *Native peoples and cultures of Canada: An anthropological overview* (2nd ed., Rev. and enlarged). Vancouver, BC: Douglas & McIntyre.

Michaelson, H. B. (1990). *How to write and publish engineering papers and reports* (3rd ed.). Phoenix, AZ: Oryx Press.

Morgan, P. P. (1983). The dupe-licators. *Canadian Medical Association Journal, 128*, 240.

Mundis, J. (1991). *Break writer's block now!* New York: St. Martin's Press.

National Research Council of Canada. (1993). A new publication policy for the NRC. *Scholarly Publishing, 24*(4), 274–280.

Natriello, G. (1996). Lessons for young scholars seeking to publish. *Teachers College Record, 97*(4), 509–517.

Nelson, V. (1993). *On writer's block: A new approach to creativity*. New York: Houghton Mifflin.

Norman, G. R., & Streiner, D. L. (1997). *PDQ statistics* (2nd ed.). St. Louis, MO: Mosby.

Norris, R. P. (1993). Authorship patterns in CJNR: 1970–1991. *Scientometrics, 28*(2), 151–158.

Oliu, W. E., Brusaw, C. T., Alred, G. J., & Scott, R. C. (1994). *Writing that works: Effective communication in business* (2nd Canadian ed.). Scarborough, ON: Nelson Canada.

Oliver, R. T. (1986). The professor as a writer. *Communication Education, 35*, 186–192.

Olson, G. A. (1997). Publishing scholarship in humanistic disciplines: Joining the conversation. In J. M. Moxley & T. Taylor (Eds.), *Writing and publishing for academic authors* (2nd ed., pp. 51–70). Lanham, MD: Rowman & Littlefield.

O'Neill, G. P., & Sachis, P. N. (1994). The importance of refereed publications in promotion and tenure decisions: A Canadian study. *Higher Education, 28*(4), 427–435.

O'Neill, G. P., & Sachis, P. N. (1998). Journal peer review: An endorsement in principle. *Higher Education in Europe, 23*(4), 517–526.

Pickett, J. P., et al. (Eds.). (2000). *The American heritage dictionary of the English language* (4th ed.). Boston, MA: Houghton Mifflin.

Prytherch, R. J. (Comp.). (2000). *Harrod's librarians' glossary and reference book* (9th ed.). Brookfield, VT: Gower.

Ressler, S. (1997). *The art of electronic publishing: The internet and beyond.* Upper Saddle River, NJ: Prentice-Hall.

Ritchie, J. A. (1997). Myths of the writing life. *The Writer, 110*(12), 21–22.

Ross, S. M., & Morrison, G. R. (1993). How to get research articles published in professional journals. *Tech Trends, 38*(2), 29–30, 32.

Royal Commission on Aboriginal Peoples. (1996). *People to people, nation to nation: Highlights from the report of the Royal Commission on Aboriginal Peoples.* Ottawa, ON: Minister of Supply and Services Canada.

Sabin, W. A., Millar, W. K., Sine, S. L., & Strashok, G. W. (1999). *The Gregg reference manual* (5th Canadian ed.). Toronto, ON: McGraw-Hill Ryerson.

Sawchuk, J. (1998). *The dynamics of native politics: The Alberta Metis.* Saskatoon, SK: Purich Publishing.

Schwartz, M., & The Task Force on Bias-free Language of the Association of American University Presses. (1995). *Guidelines for bias-free writing.* Bloomington, IN: Indiana University Press.

Sides, C. H. (1999). *How to write & present technical information* (3rd ed.). Phoenix, AZ: Oryx Press.

Smith, P. A. (1997). The art and agendas of writing a successful textbook proposal. In J. M. Moxley & T. Taylor (Eds.), *Writing and publishing for academic authors* (2nd ed., pp. 91–112). Lanham, MD: Rowman & Littlefield.

Smylie, J. (2000). A guide for health professionals working with aboriginal peoples: The sociocultural context of aboriginal peoples in Canada. *Journal SOGC, 100*, 1070–1081.

Strath, L., Avery, H., & Taylor, K. (1993). *Notes on the preparation of essays in the arts and sciences*. Peterborough, ON: Trent University, Academic Skills Centre.

Strauss, S. (1969). Guidelines for analysis of research reports. *Journal of Educational Research, 63*, 165–169.

Theilhelmer, R. (2003). How publishing can be more than not perishing: Writing relationships. *Change, 35*(2), 48–53.

Thyer, B. A. (1994). *Successful publishing in scholarly journals*. Thousand Oaks, CA: Sage.

Tichy, H. J. (1988). *Effective writing for engineers, managers, and scientists* (2nd ed.). Toronto, ON: Wiley.

Vaver, D. (2000). *Copyright law*. Toronto, ON: Irwin Law.

Williams, J. M. (1990). *Style: Toward clarity and grace*. Chicago, IL: University of Chicago Press.

Young, H. (Ed.). (1983). *The ALA (American Library Association) glossary of library and information science*. Chicago, IL: Western Publishing.

Zinsser, W. (2001). *On writing well: The classic guide to writing nonfiction* (6th ed., Rev. and updated). New York: HarperCollins.

Subject Index